ETERNAL ANSWERS

(Arrangement of Bhagavad-Gita by Topic)

Swami Parameshananda

Swami Pranavananda Institute Of Culture & Research
Bharat Sevashram Sangha
211 Rash Behari Avenue
Kolkata - 700019

Order this book online at www.trafford.com
or email orders@trafford.com

Most Trafford titles are also available at major online book retailers.

Printed in the United States of America.

ISBN: 978-1-4269-6347-6 (sc)
ISBN: 978-1-4251-5310-6 (e)

Trafford rev. 06/20/2011

North America & international
toll-free: 1 888 232 4444 (USA & Canada)
phone: 250 383 6864 ♦ fax: 812 355 4082

Published by:

Swami Pranavananda Institute of Culture & Research
211 Rash Behari Avenue
Kolkata - 700019, India
Phone: +91 33 2440-5178/2326
Email: bss_ho@vsnl.net
          bharatsevashram@gmail.com
Website: www.bharatsevashramsangha.net

Sponsored by:
ARCH AUTO PARTS
New York, U.S.A.

Sincere gratitude to:
Biswanath Debsinha, Computer Compositor
Mrs. Nandita Ghosh, Proof Reader

Printed by:
Sugg. Donation: **$ 16.00**
          Rs. 75.00

PREFACE

In this age of computer, access to information has been made simple. The younger generation, the future guardians of religion and culture, are looking for quick answers that will help them understand who is God.

People from all faiths are seeking peace in the present life and are eager to know what will happen in the after life. An interfaith conference was sponsored by Willow Creek Community Church, Chicago (the largest Church in U.S.A. for weekend attendance) in an effort to answer these questions. Although, the answers given by the worlds largest faith, Christianity, Islam, Hinduism, Buddhism and Judaism differ, their belief systems have unifying factors that includes, faith that God will deliver from the sufferings of this world.

Through the blessings of Swami Pranavananda Maharaj, I was given the opportunity to represent Hinduism. My spiritual experiences, exposures to the multifarious activities of Bharat Sevashram Sangha in India and other parts of the world, together with the teachings of the Bhagavad-Gita were my main sources for the discourse.

'Gita' is the recording of the dialogue between God, Sri Krishna and His most dear disciple, Arjuna. It is the summary and essence of Hinduism.

This book is a presentation of Bhagavad-Gita by subject matter. Mahatma Gandhi once said, "When disappointment stares me in the face and all alone I see not one ray of light, I go back to the Bhagavad-Gita, I find a verse here and a verse there and I immediately begin to smile in the midst of overwhelming tragedies". To read, contemplate and put into practice one verse can lead one to liberation. Lord Krishna said that there is no greater service to Him than to bring the teachings of Gita to the masses.

Going through the exercise of putting this book together gave me a sense of fulfillment; I hope it does the same for you.

The original information and some interpretations for the slokas have been taken from 'Srimad Bhagabad Gita' by Jagadish Ch. Ghosh and 'The Bhagavad Gita' with commentary by Swami Chidbhavananda. My sincere gratitude to them.

- Swami Parameshananda

BLESSINGS

<u>Souls on the path to liberation</u>

Swami Parameshananda is an ordained Sannyasi of Bharat Sevashram Sangha, a monastic and philanthropic organization with its Head Office located in Kolkata, India.

He has lived in New York; U.S.A. for the last 39 years and we are happy to say that his monastic life is a contribution of America. He was handpicked and nurtured by the divine lofty ideals of Sreemat Swami Pranavanandaji.

It was a pleasure to see Parameshananda develop his spiritual life by the grace of Sri Guru Maharaj, incarnation of Lord Shiva, since coming to India in 1996. His physical stamina and mental endurance make him an ideal instrument for the fulfillment of the divine mission.

I sincerely feel all will gain tremendously by reading his presentation of The Bhagavad Gita topic by topic as it addresses the eternal questions and answers.

With Blessings,

(Swami Buddhananda)
General Secretary
Bharat Sevashram Sangha
Kolkata 700019, INDIA

TABLE OF CONTENTS

Introduction of Gita

When righteousness declines and vice (immorality, impurity, persecution, exploitation, cut-throat competition and disorder) prevails in creation, then in order to root out the evils and protect the righteousness, reinstate justice and religion, peace and order, the supreme power manifests itself on earth. They are called Incarnation, Acharya, Guru, Prophet, Emancipator and Saviour etc.

In different ages and in different parts of the world these manifestations preach and propagate different ideals, inculcate different rules and ideologies according to the demand and necessity of the time. But they take incarnation with the one idea and for the same purpose. Therefore, their ideals and systems, modus operandi and procedure bear a strikingly common feature.

Sri Krishna God in the highest form of incarnation, planned His descent is in a very dramatic way. The great epic Mahabharat has all the ingredients that demonstrate the woes of society. Members of two first cousins, one righteous and the other unrighteous fought the war. Sri Krishna made all efforts to avert the war but He was not hesitant to encourage the righteous Pandavas to fight.

In 1896 the same God came again in human form as world teacher Swami Pranavananda. He took to intense austerity and at the age of twenty He rose to Godhood. Immediately thereafter, ten divine truths came out of His mouth. They became the guiding rules for the Bharat Sevashram Sangha, the monastic order that He formed. Like the Buddha, He wanted His work to spread far and wide.

The following are the **ten divine messages** –

Message of the Prophet of the age
(The essence of the Bhagavad Gita)

1. What is the Goal of Life?   -   Self-realization
Universal emancipation

2. What is religion?   -   Self-sacrifice (self-abnegation)
Self-discipline
Adherence to truth and
continence

3. What is real death?   -   Forgetfulness of the "Self"

4. What is real life?   -   Self-realization
Self-remembrance
Self-consciousness

5. What are real virtues?   -   Heroism, Virility, Manliness
and aspiration for
emancipation

6. What are real sins?   -   Weakness, Fear (Defeatism)
Cowardice, Meanness and
Selfishness

7. What are real sources of
strength?   -   Patience, Fortitude and
Endurance

8. What are real assets?   -   Self-confidence
Self-reliance
Self-respect

9. What are real enemies?   -   Indolence, Slumber, Inertia,
Procrastination, Lustful senses
and Passions

10. What are real friends?   -   Energy, Enthusiasm and
Perseverance

A question may arise - what is the necessity of Swami Pranavananda's austerity? In reply, it can be said that He has incarnated for the welfare of the human society. He must set an example. In the Geeta Lord Sri Krishna has also said, "There is nothing in the three worlds for me to do, nor is there anything worth attaining, unattained by me. Yet I continue to work. If I do not engage myself unwearied, great harm will come to the world, because men follow my path. Whatsoever a great man does other men follow that, whatever standard he sets up, the common people follow the same." (The Gita 3/21, 22,23)

Swami Pranavananda felt an urge to propagate this message in the society and wrote to one of His disciples', "The Sangha Message is some supreme Truths realized by the founder of your Sangha. In different ages great souls attain salvation and dispense the truths realized for the welfare of the humanity. This message of the Sangha is being introduced for the benefit of mankind. This should be brought home to all. Then all will be reading them daily." Once by way of advice He told a disciple of the Sangha, **"The message of the Sangha reflects all the truths of the Vedas, Vedanta, Puranas and the Great epics of the Mahabharata and the Ramayana."**

The Geeta reads, "If you prostrate yourself at the feet of the wise, render them all forms of service, and question them with a guileless heart, again and again, the wise seers of Truth will unfold the knowledge to you." So all the scriptures of India have been exposed through question and answer. This message has appeared on the same line. Swami Pranavananda asked the questions and He gave the solutions, as man does not know what he really hankers after. He who has adopted all the grief, misery, trials and turmoil of the human society as His own, can put the questions and give the answer to the point.

The Bhagavad-Gita has served Hindus and non-Hindus all over the world. It has been translated into many languages. The arrangement that you will read in this book is for today's fast moving society. It is the message eternal.

Geeta Dhyanam

(MEDITATION ON GITA)

1   *om pārthāya pratibodhitām bhagavatā nārāyanena svayam*
vyāsena grathitām purāna munina madhye mahābhāratam
advaitāmrtavarsinim bhagavatim astādasādhyāyinim
amba tvām anusandadhāmi bhagavadgite bhavadvesinim

Oh Mother Bhagawata Gita, You dwell in the words that Lord Krishna
speaks to Arjuna as recounted by the ancient sage Vyasdeva in the Bhishma
Chapter (Chapter 18/25-42 of the Mahabharata). Thou art the immortal
nectar of the 18 chapters on non-duality. Oh Mother Bhagawati - I meditate
on Thee who negates the meshes of this worldly existence.

2   *namo 'stu te vyāsa visāla buddhe*
phullāravindāyata patra netra
yena tvayā bhārata tailapūrnah
prajvālito jnānamayah pradipah

Salutations to Vyasdeva, the ocean of wisdom, with eyes akin to the
blooming lotus. You have lit the lamp of knowledge - the Mahabharata.
I bow to Thee.

3   *prananna pārijātāya*
totravetraika pānaye
jnāna mudrāya krsnāya
gitāmrta duhe namah

I bow to Sri Krishna, who to the seekers is the mythical Tree that grants boons. Driving the horses in one hand He holds the reins, while with the other He milks the nectar of knowledge from the immortal Gita.

4
sarvopanisado gāvo
dogdhā gopāla nandanah
pārtho vatsah sudhir bhoktā
dugdham gitāmrtam mahat

The Upanishads are the cows, the one who milks them is Gopala, the calf is Arjuna and the sacred milk is The Gita, the nectar of immortality.

5
vasudeva sutam devam
kamsa cānura mardanam
devaki paramānandam krsnam
vande jagad gurum

Salutations to the Lord of Creation, Sri Krishna who slew the demon Kansa and Chanur. He is the source of joy to His mother Devaki.

6
bhisma drona tatā jayadratha jalā gāndhāra
nilotpalā salya grāhavati krpena vahant karnena velākula
asvatthāma vikarna ghora makarā duryodhanāvartini
sottirnd khalu pāndavai rana nadi kaivartakah kesavah

The Kurukshetra war is the river whose two shores are Bhishma and Drona, whose waters are Jayadratha and whose slippery blue shore is King of Gandhara. Shalya is the crocodile in the current known as Kripa. Karna is the turbulent wave, Asvatthama and Bikarna are the two alligators while Duryodhana is the swirling current. With Sri Krishna at the helm as the boatman, the Pandavas could safely navigate through this ferocious river of strife.

7
pārāsarya vacah sarojam amalan
gittārtha gandhotkatam
nānākhyānaka kesaram hari kathā
sambodhanā bodhitam
loke sajjana satpadair aharahah
pepiyamānam mudā
bhuyād bhārata pankajam kalimala
pradhvamsinah sreyase

The words of sage Vyasdeva, son of Parasar, are the lotus flowers blooming with the words of Sri Hari. Its chapters are like the filaments from which the wise of this world drink the honey – the nectar that negates the evil of Kali Yuga (our present time). May the strong scent of this Lotus, of the Gita, bless us.

8

mukam karoti vācālam
angum langhayate girim
yatkrpā tam aham vande
paramānanda mādhavam

I salute Madhava, the embodiment of bliss. By His grace the dumb speak and the lame climb the mountains.

9

yam brahmā varunendra rudra marutah
stunvanti divyaih stavaih
vedaih sānga pada kramopanisadair
gāyanti yam sāmagāh
dhyānvasthita tadgatena manasā
pasyanti yam yogino
yasyāntam na viduh surāsuraganā
devāya tasmai namah

Salutations to that God whom Brahma, Varuna, Indra, Rudra and the Maruts praise with divine hymns, whose greatness is sung by the Sama Chanters through the Angas, Padkrama and the Vedas and Whom the yogins perceived in a state of intoxication. Even the Devas and Asuras are ignorant of His real nature. I salute that God of gods.

A Great Saviour and Nation Builder
Yugacharya Swami Pranavanandaji Maharaj
Founder: **Bharat Sevashram Sangha**

SRI KRISHNA
The deliverer of the message of Bhagavad Gita.
The Lord of the great epic Mahabharata

SRI KRISHNA AS THE CREATOR
*As His past time, He created the universe with only
a small fraction of His power (See page 41)*

**SRI CHAITANYA MAHAPRABHU,
GOURANGA AND CLOSE FOLLOWERS**
The embodiment of devotion through constant chanting praises to the Lord

LORD SHIVA

LORD BUDDHA

The incarnation of the Cosmic Consciousness. (See Chapter 3)

A YOGI LEAVING HIS BODY

With breath control and six power centers, the yogi can move his life force to the top of his head. Then it leaves from the top of his head and merges with the Cosmic Will at the time of death (See Page 159)

THE ILLUSION OF LUST

*Who have little knowledge they seek to fufill their carnal hankerings.
Demigods cannot fulfill the desires of devotees unless the Lord sanctions
them. (See Chapter 4)*

LIFE-DEATH CYCLE

The body undergoes changes constantly as it moves from babe to old age and then it falls off from the permanent soul at death. (See Chapter V)

SRI ADI SHANKARACHARYA

The reviver of ancient Hinduism through the establishment of monastic ashram

MOTHER DURGA

The symbol of power as She received weapons from primary Gods.
(See Page 27)

UNIVERSAL COSMIC FORM

Seeing the universal form of the Lord, all of Arjuna's doubts vanished.
He then prostrated in front of the Lord. (See Page 11)

CHAPTER - I

What is God like?

Consciousness

7-7

*mattah parataram nā 'nyat
kimcid asti dhananjaya
mayi sarvam idam protam
sutre maniganā iva*

O Dhananjaya (Arjuna), there is nothing whatever that excels me. All that is here is threaded on Me like gems held together on a thread.

In one image of God He appears as half man and half woman so as to make Himself knowable. This form indicates that He is the creator and also the created. Beings and things in creation look different but they are all united by Pure Consciousness.

7-26

*vedā 'ham samatitāni
vartamānāni cā 'rjuna
bhavisyāmi ca bhutāni
mām tu veda na kascana*

I know, O Arjuna, the beings of the past, the present and the future, but no one knows Me.

Just as the swan can separate milk from water and then drink the former, the Paramahansas – perfected souls, are able to remove worldly illusion (Maya) then the Lord is visible.

8-4   *adhibhutam ksharo bhāvah*
                       purushas cā 'dhidaivatam
                       adhiyajno 'ham evā 'tra
                       dehe dehabhritām vara

O Best of All Embodied Beings (Arjuna), all perishable objects are adhibhuta, the purusha (Brahman) is adhidaivata and in this body, I am the adhiyajna.

adhibhuta - is the five elements.

adhidaivata - is the cosmic soul.

adhiyajna - is the Lord. Vishnu Bhagawan, He is the receiver of sacrifices.

The five elements ether, air, fire, water and earth serve as the embodiment of the Jivatmans (the rays of the Cosmic Consciousness, the soul). They are temporary while the seed in the fruit (Jivatma) lives on. Sacrifice or the surrendering of one individual self creates divinity and as such God is present. Total surrender is the ultimate surrender or sacrifice.

8-20   *paras tasmāt tu bhāvo 'nyo*
                       'vyakto 'vyaktāt sanātanah
                       yah sa sarvesu bhuteshu
                       nashyatsu na vinasyati

But beyond this unmanifested, there is yet another Unmanifested Eternal Existence which does not perish even when all existence perishes.

9-4   *mayā tatam idam sarvam*
                       jagad avaktamurtinā
                       matsthāni sarvabhutāni
                       na cā 'ham teshu avasthitah

I pervade this entire universe remaining unmanifested. All beings dwell in Me but I do not dwell in them.

As waves take their origin from the ocean but the ocean is not contained in them, Brahman the unmanifested God, is not affected by what is manifested.

9-6

yathā 'kasasthito nityam
vāyuh sarvatrago mahān
tathā sarvāni bhutāni
matsthāni 'ty upadhāraya

As the air, vast and always moving everywhere, abides in the expanse of ether, so all beings, know thou this, exist in Me.

9-17

pitā 'ham asya jagato
mātā dhātā pitāmahah
vedyam pavitram omkāra
rik sāma yajur eva ca

I am the father of this world, the mother, the sustainer and the grandsires. I am the goal of knowledge, the purifier. I am the syllable Om and I am the Sama, Rik and Yajus Vedas as well.

10-2

na me viduh suraganāh
prabhavam na maharshayah
aham ādir hi devānām
maharshinām ca sarvashah

Neither the Gods nor the great sages are aware of My origin for I am the primal source of them in all respects.

10-8

aham sarvasya prabhavo
mattah sarvam pravartate
iti matvā bhajante mām
budhā bhāvasamanvitāh

I am the origin of all. From Me does everything evolve. Knowing this the wise, filled with love and devotion, worship me.

Constant thinking of God enriches the mind and makes one a Yogi.

10-12

arjuna uvāca
param brahma param dhāma
pavitram paramam bhavān
purusham shāshvatam divyam
ādidevam ajam vibhum

Thou art the Supreme Brahman, the Supreme Abode and the Supreme Purifier, the Eternal, Divine Person, the First of the Gods, the Unborn and the All-pervading.

10-15   *svayam evā 'tmanā 'tmānam*
                      vettha tvam purushottama
                      bhutabhāvana bhutesha
                      devadeva jagatpate

O Supreme Being, source of life and Lord, the God of Gods, the Lord of the world, Thou, Thyself alone, knowest what Thou art by the light of Thy knowledge.

The glory of the Lord is perceived based on the power of the understanding of the individual, in the same way a precious stone is given value by people who are unfamiliar with it. Individual souls are called Purushas because they have to vacate the body after Mukti. But the Lord is the ruler and God over His creations.

10-22   *vedānām sāmavedo 'smi*
                      devānām asmi vāsavah
                      indriyānām manas cā 'smi
                      bhutānām asmi cetanā

Among the Vedas, I am the Samaveda; among the gods, I am Indra; among the senses, I am the mind; and I am consciousness in living beings.

Sama Veda is written and chanted in musical tone so it invites bhakti. The mind being the recorder of all sensations is superior to the senses.

10-39   *yac cā 'pi sarvabhutānām*
                      bijam tad aham arjuna
                      na tad asti vinā yat syān
                      mayā bhutam carācaram

O Arjuna, I am further the seed of all beings; there is nothing moving or inert that can exist without Me.

10-42   *athavā bahunai 'tena*
                 kim jnātena tava 'rjuna
                 vishtabhyā 'ham idam kritsnam
                 ekāmshena sthito jagat

But what do you stand to gain, O Arjuna, by knowing all this in detail? I remain sustaining this entire universe by only a portion of Myself.

The waves are an insignificant aspect of the vast ocean, yet someone looking from the shores sees the waves as everything. In the same way, creation is but a small fraction of God. Only God knows Himself.

11-18   **tvam aksharam paramam veditavyam**
                 tvam asya vishvasya param nidhānam
                 tvam avyayah shāshvatadharmagoptā
                 sanātanas tvam purusho mato me

Thou art the Imperishable, the Supreme One, who is to be realized. Thou art the final refuge in the universe. Thou art the deathless champion of the eternal law (Dharma). To me Thou art the Eternal Person.

You are both Brahman and Isvara absolute.

Sasvatadharma Gupta - guardian of the eternal law.

11-38   **tvam ādidevah purushah purānas**
                 tvam asya vishvasya param nidhānam
                 vettā 'si vedyam ca param ca dhāma
                 tvayā tatam vishvam anantarupa

O Thou of the Infinite Form, Thou art the Prime Deity, the Ancient Purusha, the Supreme Resort of the World. Thou art the Knower, the Knowable, and the Supreme Goal. It is Thee who pervades the universe.

You are the first and oldest occupant of your creation, Prakriti. At the end of every cycle, what was created goes back to You, Oh God.

11-43   **pitāsi lokasya carācarasya**
                 tvam asya pujyas ca gurur gariyān
                 na tvatsamo'sty abhyadhikah kuto'nyo
                 lokatraye'py apratima-prabhāva

Father, Thou art of the universe, moving and unmoving. Thou art the one to be worshipped and the most solemn object of veneration. None is equal to Thee. How can there be one superior to Thee in the three worlds, O Thou Incomparable in Might?

The supreme is one; no other can be in the same level with Him.

13-12   *jneyam yat tat pravakshyāmi*
                   yaj jnātva'mritam ashnute
                   anādi matparam brahma
                   na sat tannā'sad ucyate

I will now describe what one should know and knowing which one will attain to life eternal. It is Brahman, My attributeless aspect, without beginning or end and said to be neither existent nor non-existent.

God is manifested and unmanifested. The three gunas cause variations in the manifested state but when these three gunas are in equilibrium the manifested state ceased to exist. Nirgun Brahman or Pure Consciousness is ever constant, there is no beginning and no end as there is neither manifestation or unmanifestation. Great souls can realize this state through meditation. After which the need for enquiry into knowledge and ignorance (Purusha and Prakriti) ends.

The effect of evolving in wisdom (13-15)

13-13   *sarvatah pānipādam tat*
                   sarvatokshi-shiromukham
                   sarvatah shrutimalloke
                   sarvamāvritya tishthati

Everywhere is His hands and feet. His eyes, heads and faces are on all sides and everywhere are His ears. He remains encompassing all.

13-14   *sarvendriya gunābhāsam*
                   sarvendriya vivarjitam
                   asaktam sarvabhric cai'va
                   nirgunam gunabhoktri ca

He seems to have the functions of the senses and is yet devoid of the senses, is unattached and yet sustains everything, is unaffected by the gunas (qualities) and yet enjoys them.

God and His creation are inseparable. He gives the five senses their brilliance. The gunas are not part of Brahman but yet they are projected on Him as He is all pervading and so appears, as he is the gunas. In the same way a screen reflexes the actions of a film but remains the same.

13-15   **bahir antas ca bhutānām**
                     acaram caram eva ca
                     sukshmatvāt tadavijneyam
                     durastham cā'ntike ca tat

He exists without and within all beings, He is unmoving and also moving, He is beyond grasp being too subtle. He is utterly distant and yet so near.

Although Pure Consciousness is not an element, it is all pervading. It does not need rest. Consciousness or Brahma can be compared to sunlight. It seems to have form and color but it does not. It is like a screen in a theatre. On it all the actions are happening but it is not affected. The three qualities (gunas) of man act because of God Consciousness. God and His creation are inseparable.

One appearing as the many (16 & 17)

13-16   **avibhaktam ca bhuteshu**
                     vibhaktam iva ca sthitam
                     bhuta bhartri ca taj jneyam
                     grasishnu prabhavishnu ca

Though indivisible, He is parceled out among beings. Know Him to be the sustainer, destroyer and creator of all beings.

It is the same universal consciousness that becomes the individual soul but it is not divided. At the end of one day of existence all the individual souls return and creation no longer exists. At the end of the night they reappear.

13-17   *jyotishām api taj jyotis*
                                   tamasah param ucyate
                                   jnānam jneyam jnānagamyam
                                   hridi sarvasya vishthitam

He is the light of all lights and is said to be beyond darkness (ignorance). He is knowledge itself, object of knowledge and attainable through knowledge. He dwells in all hearts.

The sun and moon glow, the earth bustles with life, but at the end of a day of Brahman (Kalpa) they cease to exist because they are powered by the universal God. Absence of light in a dark room, is the same as when one is in meditation (eyes closed), he is aware of his being because of the all illuminating soul. The perceptive senses, the thinking mind and the reasoning intellect gets its lumination from the cosmic consciousness or the Atma. One must realize that ultimate truth exists inside. Only then he or she will see God in all of creation.

14-4   *sarva yonishu kaunteya*
                                   murtayah sambhavanti yāh
                                   tāsām brahma mahad yonir
                                   aham bijapradah pitā

O Son of Kunti (Arjuna), whatever forms are born of wombs, great Prakriti is the womb and I am the father who plants the seed.

15-4   *tatah padam tat parimārgitavyam*
                                   yasmin gatā na nivartanti bhuyah
                                   tam eva cā'dyam purusham prapadye
                                   yatah pravrittih prasritā purāni

Then, that path must be sought from which those who have reached it never return, saying, "I seek refuge only in that Primal Person from whom has come forth this ancient current of the world" (this cosmic process).

Detachment from the world without creating the replacement by diligently seeking to merge the individual soul with the cosmic consciousness is no good. It is like moving from a house to an ashram. It elevates by going to where godliness is ever present. When the sadhaka sees and realizes the play of Maya, it ceases to exist just like when a thief is detected he runs away.

15-15   *sarvasya cāham hridi sannivishto*
           mattah smritir jnānam apohanam ca
           vedais ca sarvair aham eva vedyo
           vedāntakrid vedavid eva cāham

I dwell in everybody's heart; memory and knowledge proceed from Me and lose themselves in Me. It is I Whom the Vedas seek to know. I am the author and knower of the Vedanta.

Memory - the faculty of recollecting past events, knowledge - the faculty to reacting to a changing world, comes from consciousness (God without form). So also is lost of unwanted retention of memory. Knowledge of cosmic functions is known as Vedas. Cosmic functions are the revelations of the all pervading nature. Vedanta is knowing that God exists beyond nature (Prakriti).

15-16   *dvāvimau purushau loke*
           ksharashcā kshara eva ca
           ksharah sarvani bhutāni
           kutastho'kshara ucyate

In this world, there are two kinds of purushas (entities)- perishable and imperishable. All beings are perishable. The changeless one is said to be imperishable.

Just as the temporary waves have an identity of realness and fuse again with the endless ocean so the Jivatma or individual consciousness fuse with the absolute consciousness once it losses its identity. The original consciousness was never and never will be under the control of Maya.

15-17   *uttamah purushas tvanyah*
           paramātmety udāhritah
           yo lokatrayam āvishya
           bibharty avyaya ishvarah

There is the Supreme Person distinct from these called the Supreme Self. It is He Who as the imperishable Lord, pervading the three worlds, and sustaining all.

God is everything and the master of this illusionary world.(We can recognize Him in our Souls and all that is this world.) In His higher form He can be called pure consciousness and awareness. For study purposes He is called Mahanarayan, Sadasiva and Parasakti.

15-18   ***yasmāt ksharam atito'ham***
                         aksharād api cottamah
                         ato'smi loke vede ca
                         prathitah purushottamah

Since I transcend the perishable and excel the imperishable, I am known in the Vedas and in this world as the Supreme Person (Purushottama).

Kshara connotes what is perishable. All of creation is perishable. The false identification of the individual soul with creation or nature is perishable but the pure consciousness of the original cosmic self is not perishable. Realized souls can understand this.

Universal (cosmic) form

11-7
ihai'kastham jagat kritsnam
pashyā'dya sacarācaram
mama dehe gudākesha
yac cā'nyad drashtum icchasi

Behold here today, O Gudakesa, the whole universe of the moving and the unmoving, and whatever else you desire to see, all integral of My body.

11-8
na tu mām shakyase drashtum
anenai 'va svacakshusha
divyam dadāmi te cakshuh
pashya me yogam aishvaram

But thou canst behold Me with these eyes of yours. I give to Thee the divine vision. Behold my marvelous power.

Man with all his progressive mastery over the knowledge of nature has not solved the problems of life and death. Spiritual life fills this void or mystery. Through the grace of God, the spiritual aspirant merges his personal will with that of the cosmic will, thereby becoming a God realized soul. Intuition or the third eye is the fruit of this union. God realization in the various planes of the consciousness –

1. *Mental plain - the phenomenon*
2. *Ethical plain - infallible law*
3. *Divine eye level - kinetic or active God*
4. *Intuitive level - static God*

After these levels, the individuals merge with God. Arjuna was bestowed by God's grace the divine eye and so all his problems disappeared.

11-11
divya mālyāmbara dharam
divya gandhānulepanam
sarvāshcaryamayam devam
anantam vishvatomukham

That Divine Form wearing divine garlands and garments, besmeared with ointments divinely perfumed, supremely wondrous, resplendent and boundless has His face turning in all directions.

The spectacle that we enjoy in God's creation is mind-boggling. It can only be perceived with the third eye.

11-12   *divi surya sahasrasya*
                                        bhaved yugapad utthitā
                                        yadi bhāh sadrsi sā
                                        syād bhāsas tasya mahātmanah

If the splendor of a thousand suns were to blaze forth all at once in the sky, that would be like the splendor of that Mahatman.

11-13   *tatrai 'kastham jagat kritsnam*
                                        pravibhaktam anekadhā
                                        apashyad deva devasya
                                        sharire pāndavas tadā

There the Pandava (Arjuna) saw the entire universe with its many ramifications, massed together in one, in the body of the God of gods.

Arjuna saw unity and variety coming together in Sri Krishna as the universal self. It is God's plan to unify the various planes of enjoyment as they all exist in Him.

11-15   *arjuna uvāca*
                                        pashyami devāms tava devadehe
                                        sarvāms tathā bhuta vishesha samghān
                                        brahmānam isham kamalāsanastham
                                        rishims ca sarvān uragāms ca divyān

In Thy body, O Lord, I see all the Gods and all the groups of various beings, Brahma the Lord seated on the lotus and all the sages and the divine serpents.

Isha is here referred to Brahman with four faces.

11-16   *aneka bāhudara vaktra netram*
                                        pasyāmi tvām sarvato 'nantarupam
                                        nā 'ntam na madhyam na punas tavā 'dim
                                        pasyāmi visvesvara visvarupa

I behold You, infinite in forms on all sides, with countless arms, stomachs, mouths and eyes; neither Your end nor the middle nor the beginning do I see, O Lord of the universe, O Universal Form.

11-19 *nādi madhyāntam ananta viryam*
ananta bāhum sasi surya netram
pasyāmi tvām dipta hutāsa vaktram
svatejasā visvam idam tapantam

I see You without beginning, middle or end and infinite in power. I see you with infinite arms, the sun and the moon being Your eyes, the burning fire Your mouth heating the whole universe with Your radiance.

11-21 *ami hi tvām surasamghā vishanti*
kecid bhitāh prānjalayo grinanti
svasti 'ty uktvā maharshi-siddhasamghāh
stuvanti tvām stutibhih pushkalābhih

Verily these hosts of Gods all enter into Thee. Some in fear are invoking Thy protection, with folded hands. Hosts of great sages (Maharshis) and perfected ones (Siddhas) chanting 'Swasti' (Let there be peace, may it be well) are extolling Thee by singing Thy highest praises.

The great souls like Narada and Kapila always pray by saying "Lord may good come out of your great deeds". Mass destruction of God's creation is His way of cleaning the world of wickedness. Realized souls humbly accept this with folded hands and in prayer.

11-22 *rudrāditya vasavo ye ca sādhyā*
vishve 'shvinau marutash co'smapāsh ca
gandharva yakshāsura siddhasamghā
vikshante tvām vismitāsh cai'va sarve

The Rudras, the Ādityas, the Vasus, the Sadhyas, the two Asvins, the Maruts, the Manes and the hosts of Gandharvas, Yakshas, Asuras and Siddhas, all gaze at Thee, utterly amazed.

The celestials have some knowledge of the plan of God but at the sight of mass destruction (in the universal form of God), they also are humbled.

11-25   *damshtrākarālāni ca te mukhāni*
                    drishtvai'va kālānalasannibhāni
                    disho na jāne na labhe ca sharma
                    prasida devesha jagannivāsa

O Lord of Gods, seeing Thy mouths with their fearful fangs, looking like
the raging flames when the world cometh to an end, I lose my bearings
and all content. Be gracious, O Refuge of the worlds.

The fright that was caused by the glow emanating from the Lord made Arjuna
crave to see the Lord's peaceful form. He wanted now to see the Sun with
its brightness on beautiful earths and no longer the terrible light he has seen
coming from the Lord.

11-31   *ākhyāhi me ko bhavān ugrarupo*
                    namo 'stu te devavara prasida
                    vijnātum icchāmi bhavantam ādyam
                    na hi prajānāmi tava pravrittim

Tell me who Thou art in this terrible form. I bow to Thee, O Thou Great
Lord, be gracious. I seek to know Thee, the Primal Being, for I know not
the ways of Thy working.

The devotee should worship God in all of His forms as He has no limitations.
Arjuna is starting to realize this. Fear is overcome by worshipping of the fearful
but Arjuna is doing this with hesitation.

11-39   *vāyur yamo 'gnir varunah shashānkah*
                    prajāpatis tvam prapitāmahashca
                    namo namas te 'stu sahasrakritvah
                    punash ca bhuyo 'pi namo namaste

I hail to Thee a thousand times who art Vayu (the wind), Yama (the God
of destruction), Agni (Fire), Varuna (the Sea-God) and Shashanka (the
moon). My salutations to Thee who art the Lord of Creation (Brahma)
and the Supreme grandsire. I bow to Thee again and again.

Arjuna realizes Lord Krishna is everything Even Brahma came from Him.
His devotion for the Lord was increasing.

11-40
> *namah purastād atha prishthatas te*
> *namo 'stu te sarvata eva sarva*
> *anantaviryāmitavikramas tvam*
> *sarvam samāpnoshi tato 'si sarvah*

Hail to Thee from before and from behind. O Soul of All, hail to Thee from all sides, O Thou who possesseth infinite prowess and boundless might; Thou pervadest all, hence Thou art all.

Service to humanity is service to the Lord. Having the vision of the Lord in a specific form is limited knowledge of Him but recognizing him in all of his creation is the true panoramic vision.

11-44
> *tasmāt pranamya pranidhāya kāyam*
> *prasādaye tvām aham isham idyam*
> *piteva putrasya sakheva sakhyuh*
> *priyah priyāyārhasi deva sodhum*

Therefore, O Lord, I bow down before Thee and prostrate my self, I pray for Thy grace. Thou Adorable Lord, It behoves Thee to bear with my fault as a father does with his son's, a friend with his friend's, a lover with that of his beloved.

Arjuna's devotion and love for the Lord continues to rise rapidly. He makes comparisons to various relationship so that he gives complete description of His sweet and charming love.

11-45
> *adrishtapurvam hrishito'smi drishtvā*
> *bhayena ca pravyathitam mano me*
> *tad eva me darshaya deva rupam*
> *prasida devesha jagannivāsha*

I have seen what was never seen before, and I feel delighted, but my mind is tormented by fear. O Godhead, show me that other form of Thine, O Lord of the Gods, O Refuge of the World. Be gracious.

The universal form of the Lord was shown to Arjuna so that he was relieved of his war problems. Once this was realized he requested Sri Krishna to return to the placid and pleasant cosmic form.

11-48   *na vedayajnādhyayanair na dānair*
                  na ca kriyābhir na tapobhir ugraih
                  evam rupah shakya aham nriloke
                  drashtum tvadanyena kurupravira

O great hero of the Kurus (Arjuna), I cannot be seen in this form in
this mortal world through the study of the Vedas, or practice of rituals,
sacrifices or severe austerities, or by any one else other than thee.

*Arjuna by surrendering to the Lord, received in return an abundance of His
grace. All rituals and academic learning are good for spiritual life but are
tainted with egoism.*

11-52   *sri bhagavān uvāca*
              sudurdarsham idam rupam
                drishtavān asi yan mama
                 devā apy asya rupasya
              nityam darshanakānkshinah

The Blessed Lord said:This form of Mine which thou hast seen is very
difficult to see. Even the Gods always long to see this form.

*No one can receive knowledge of God unless he grants His grace. Arjuna has
seen the universal form of God and so considered higher than the Devas.*

Individual Soul

2-12

> *na tvevāham jātu nā 'sam*
> *na tvam ne 'me janādhipāh*
> *na cai 'va na bhavishyāmah*
> *sarve vayam atah param*

Nor I, nor you, nor any of these ruling princes was ever non-existent before; nor is it that we shall cease to be in the future.

2-16

> *nā 'sato vidyate bhāvo*
> *nā 'bhāvo vidyate satah*
> *ubhayor api dristo 'ntas*
> *tvanayos tattvadarshibhih*

The unreal does not endure, the real is never extinguished. The seers of truth have searched both of these to the bottom.

Life is a series of experiments and experiences. At one time what seems to be ideal, after it is investigated and understood it no longer holds-up as the ideal as it is temporary. The holy ones have realized this truth after a series of such experiments and they seek to find the beginning of this fleeting world of creation. They ultimately looked within for they realized that satisfying the senses is an endless ever-increasing thing. The mundane man thinks he is the body. The Atma is real; it is not made of anything. It was in the beginning, it is now and it shall be in the end.

2-17

> *avināshi tu tad viddhi*
> *yena sarvam idam tatam*
> *vināsham avyayasyā 'sya*
> *na kascit kartum arhati*

All this is pervaded by something. Know that to be imperishable. There is none who can cause destruction to this immutable being.

Space is the subtlest of the five elements. In it all the other elements are active and ever changing. Like space, the soul has not the capacity or need to change. It is always a witness.

2-18

antavanta ime dehā
nityasyo 'ktāh sharirinah
anāshino 'prameyasya
tasmād yudhyasva bhārata

It is said that all these bodies in which dwell the imperishable, indefinable and the eternal *atman* are by themselves perishable. Therefore fight, O Bharata.

In the presence of the Lord of what good is there for Arjuna to compromise, he must fight for his salvation. It is a blessed thing to lose his temporary cage of flesh and bone upon the instruction of the Lord.

Swami Pranavanandaji gave the same instructions to His monk disciples "Shed every drop of blood if you have to uphold the ideal of this ancient righteousness that is sustaining this great organization of Bharat Sevashram Sangha."

2-19

ya enam vetti hantāram
yas cai 'nam manyate hatam
ubhau tau na vijanito
nā 'yam hanti na hanyate

Both those who know it (the soul) to be the slayer and those who know it to be slain are ignorant. It neither slays nor is slain.

2-20

na jāyate mriyate vā kadāchin
nā 'yam bhutvā bhavitā vā na bhuyah
ajo nityah shāshvato 'yam purāno
na hanyate hanyamāne sharire

This (soul) is neither born nor does it die. Nor does it exist being born. It is birth-less, immutable, eternal and primeval. Even though the body is slain, the soul is not.

To born, to exist, to grow, to change, to decay, to perish - these are the changes that the body undergoes but Atma remains the same.

2-21

vedā vināshinam nityam
ya enam ajam avyayam
katham sa purushah pārtha
kam ghātayati hanti kam

O Partha (Arjuna), how can a man who knows the soul to be imperishable, eternal, not bound by birth or decay, contrive to have anyone slain or slay him?

For the mundane man, each individual is a separate entity and his perception and reaction is limited to just that. However, for the realized soul, everything is linked together by the all pervading and all knowing Consciousness. He evaluates the stages of evolution and then reacts in an effort to assist the individual in his evolution if the situation permits.

2-22   ***vāsāmsi jirnāni yathā vihāya***
                navāni grihnāti naro 'parāni
                tathā sharirāni vihāya jirnāny
                anyāni samyāti navāni dehi

Just as a man puts off old worn-out clothes to put on new ones, so does the soul put away the worn-out body to take on a new one.

2-23   ***nai 'nam chhindanti shastrāni***
                nai 'nam dahati pāvakah
                na cai 'nam kledayānti apo
                na shoshayati mārutah

This soul cannot be slashed by weapon nor burnt by fire. It cannot be drenched by water nor dried up by air.

Except for Akasa, which is action-less, the other four elements do not affect the atman , as it is subtler. Likewise, chid-akasa or consciousness cannot be changed.

2-24   ***acchedyo 'yam adāhyo 'yam***
                akledyo 'shoshya eva ca
                nityo sarvagatah sthānur
                achalo 'yam sanātanah

This soul can neither cleave, burn, drench nor dry. It is said to be eternal, all pervasive, changeless, immovable, primeval, indescribable, and unthinkable and not subject to decay.

2-25   *avyakto 'yam acintyo 'yam*
                       avikāryo 'yam ucyate
                       tasmād evam viditvai 'nam
                       nā 'nusocitum arhasi

The Atman is said to be unmanifisted,untinkable and immutable. Therefore, knowing it as such, you should not grieve.

The definition of unmanifested is when a thing cannot be perceived by the senses.

Mutable means it can undergo changes. Atman is unchangeable so it is immutable; it is always in its original state. The element Akasa is immutable. If the atman or true self is perfect and unchangeable, why worry?

Atma is everywhere in totality and so it is immovable. Time has no effect on it so it is eternal. For the purified mind, a concept of Atma is clear as he has made relationship with it and on his journey, realizes that he is "That".

2-28   *avyaktādini bhutāni*
                       vyaktamdhyāni bhārata
                       avyakta nidhanāni eva
                       tatra kā paridevana

O Bharata (Arjuna), all beings remain unmanifest before birth and they become unmanifest after death; only in between they are manifested. Thus is there anything to lament?.

2-29   *āshcaryavat pashyati kascid enam*
                       āsharyavad vadati tathai 'va cā 'nyah
                       āshcaryavac cai 'nam anyah shrinoti
                       shrutvā apy enam veda na cai 'va kascit

Some perceive the soul as a marvel, some describe it as a marvel and some hear it reported as a marvel. But in spite of hearing about it, none can know it.

The Atma is only accessible to those who are willing to pay the price of self-discipline, steadfastness and nonattachment. Of the few that try, only a small percentage succeed, the rest suffer from doubts and so fall by the way side.

2-30
dehi nityam avadhyo 'yam
dehe sarvasya bhārata
tasmāt sarvāni bhutāni
na tvam shocitum arhasi

O Bharata (Arjuna), the soul that dwells in a body is eternal and cannot be slain. Thou shouldst not, therefore, grieve for any being.

3-17
yas tv ātmaratir eva syād
ātmatriptas ca mānavah
ātmany eva ca samtustas
tasya kāryam na vidyate

But he who delights in the self-only, who is content with self, who is happy with the self has no duty to be done.

Actions are constantly going on in the mind while the soul is always action less. As the senses feed the mind, it increases in-action. Tuned towards the atman, its activities diminish and eventually come to an action-less state. Upon transcending the world of karma, the aspirant imbibes the characteristics of the atman, bliss and peace. Glow emanates from the aspirant.

3-18
nai 'va tasya krtenā 'rtho
nā 'krtene 'ha kascana
na cā 'sya sarvabhutesu
kascid arthavyapāsrayah

For him there is in this world no object to acquire by doing an action; nor is there any loss by not doing an action; nor has he to depend on anybody for anything.

3-42
indriyāni parāny āhur
indriyebhyah param manah
manasas tu parā buddhir
yo buddheh paratas tu sah

The senses are said to be superior (to the body). The mind is superior to the senses. Superior to the mind is intellect. What, however, is superior to the intellect is He (the Ātman).

Freedom is determined by what governs our actions. When we act at the prompting of the senses we are the least free. If we reason with our intellect we are even freer and if we surrender to the Almighty Will then freedom is at its maximum.

13-23
upadrashtā 'numantā ca
bhartā bhoktā maheshvarah
paramātme 'ti cā 'pyukto
dehe 'smin purushah parah

The Supreme Spirit (dwelling) in this body is said to be the witness, sanctioner, sustainer, experiencer, Lord of lords and Supreme Self.

Upadrishta - *spectator. The Lord or the Atma observes our every thought, word or deed.*

Anumanta - *the Lord permits what is conducive to the salvation of the Jivatma.*

Bharta - *the Lord supports or gives approval or goodness.*

Bhokta - *although we may think that we have separate entity it is but only the Lord who is experiencing- the Jivatman.*

Maheswara - *the great Lord Nature or Prakriti is totally at the command of God just as a traditional Hindu housewife totally surrenders her will to her husband as she knows her liberation will come in this kind of relationship.*

13-32
anāditvān nirgunatvāt
paramātmā 'yam avyayah
sharirastho 'pi kaunteya
na karoti na lipyate

O Son of Kunti (Arjuna), being without beginning and without attributes (Gunas), the Supreme Self is immutable and though He dwells in the body, He performs no action nor is affected by the fruits of action.

Brahman is the first or supreme original Consciousness. Creation of Prakriti came afterwards at the will and the dominance of Brahman. Prakriti is ever active because of the Gunas. Prakriti or the active part of God cannot affect his inactive static aspect or un-manifested state. It was, is or will be perfection.

13-33   *yathā sarvagatam saukshmyād*
                    ākāsham nopalipyate
                    sarvatrā 'vasthito dehe
                    tathā 'tmā no 'palipyate

Like ether (Akasa) pervading all things, too subtle for taint, the Self inhabits all bodies and remains free from taint.

Just as Akasa is not tainted by the remaining four elements, Brahman or pure consciousness cannot be modified by nature; it is completely detached yet it controls nature.

Object of worship

INCARNATIONS

4-5
             sri bhagavān uvāca
             bahuni me vyatitani
             janmāni tava cā 'rjuna
             tāny aham veda sarvāni
             na tvam vettha paramtapa

The Blessed Lord said:O Arjuna, both thou and I have passed through many a life. I know all of them, thou dost not, O Chastiser of thy Foe (Arjuna).

Here the difference between an incarnation and the Jivatman comes into play. An incarnation is the manifestation of the cosmic consciousness whereas the Jivatma is a soul that is smeared by the karma on the path to cosmic consciousness. Krishna Bhagawan sat-chid-anand knows the past, present and future. Arjuna is lead by his senses and reacted with the circumstances around him.

4-6
             ajo 'pi sann avyayātmā
             bhutānām isvaro 'pi san
             prakritim svām adhisthāya
             sambhavāmy ātmamāyayā

I am not bound by the cycles of birth, I am immortal and Lord of all beings. Yet remaining steadfast in my own nature, I come into being through my own divine power (Maya, mysterious power).

The play of nature or creation is a stage for both God and man. Lord Krishna controlled her (Prakriti) actions while Arjuna is a slave to Maya Sakti (illusion). The Lord creates the universe in the same manner as he manifests Himself. God has nothing to gain as He is the architect and assumes form to be a role model.

4-7
yadā-yadā hi dharmashya
glānir bhavati bhārata
abhyutthānam adharmasya
tadā 'tmānam srijāmy aham

Whenever righteousness declines and unrighteousness thrives, O Bharata (Arjuna), I incarnate myself.

Evolution of the soul is a steady process towards perfection or liberation. Whenever this process is in jeopardy of stagnation, the creator (God) comes and gives a push-start.

4-8
paritrānāya sādhunām
vināshāya ca dushkritām
dharmasamsthā panārthāya
sambhavāmi yuge-yuge

For protecting the virtuous, for destroying the wicked and for setting righteousness on firm foundations, I am born and reborn from age to age.

When the bad exceeds the good then the Creator restores the balance through mass destruction causing war, pestilence, famine etc. The function of the incarnations is to induce goodness (Sattvika) into the hearts of the masses so as to strike a balance of the three natures of man (three gunas).

4-9
janma karma ca me divyam
evam yo vetti tattvatah
tyaktvā deham punarjanma
nai 'ti mām eti so 'rjuna

He who understands my divine birth and activities in their true nature, O Arjuna, is no longer subject to re-birth but comes to me.

The holy man who catches the spirit of truth of the Lord and His drama, transgresses the illusion of creation. He becomes lesser and lesser affected by worldly affairs while in the cage of flesh and bones. In this life He gradually merges with pure consciousness, thereby having no need to return to this world after death. The Gods and Goddesses that we worship were once Jivatmans but now are perfected souls. It is for this reason we worship holy men and women as we see God-like qualities in them. Only a few understand the incarnations and they pass this knowledge to the masses.

7-29   **jarāmaranamokshāya**
mām āshritya yatanti ye
te brahma tad viduh dritsnam
adhyātmam karma cā 'khilam

Those who strive for freedom from death and infirmities of age, taking refuge in Me, know the Brahman (Absolute), the Self an all action.

For a mind that is unwilling to follow the path of realization, death and decay are staring him in the face. These two factors are constant reminders. Contemplation on them alerts man of the goal of life.

*Swami Pranavanandaji, the Guru of Bharat Sevashram Sangha upon receiving God realization, uttered the ten divine messages of which self-realization is the first (**See Introduction to Gita**). During His short earthly sojourn He spent many nights at the cremation ground deep in meditation so as to teach mankind to think of the ultimate end of this cage of flesh and bones.*

9-11   **avajānanti mām mudhā**
mānushim tanum āsritam
param bhāvam ajānanto
mama bhutamaheshvaram

The deluded despise Me in human body, not knowing My higher nature as Lord of all existences.

Ether (Akasa) is not affected by the other four elements, although they dwell in it. It goes beyond eternity. Likewise the Lord should not be limited to His human forms as He is creation and also the all-pervading consciousness. He takes this form so that He can communicate on the human level and deliver His message of Moksha.

Personal God and Demigod

2-2
sri bhagavāna uvāca
kutas tvā kashmalam idam
vishame samupasthitam
anāryajustam asvargyam
akirtikaram arjuna

The Blessed Lord said:O Arjuna, whence hast come to thee at this hour of crisis this strange fit so unbecoming of the noble Aryan, causing the loss of heaven in the life beyond and inglorious in itself.

Up to this point, the Lord stayed quiet and listened to Arjuna's sorrow and confusion. Sri Krishna now took it upon Himself to assist Arjuna and the rest of mankind to overcome the misconception of what is real and permanent versus what is temporary.

"Om Purnamada Purnamidam Purnat Purnamadaucyate Purnasya Purnamadaya Purnamebabashiyate".

He wants Arjuna to adhere to righteousness and that of an Aryan, one of noble birth and behavior. Arjuna's state of mind made him incompetent for this world, let alone the after world.

2-3
klaibyam mā sma gamah pārtha
nai 'tat tvayy upapadyate
kshudram hridaya-daurbalyam
tyaktvo 'ttstha paramtapa

O Partha (Arjuna), do not be down-hearted. Such unmanliness is unbecoming of thee. O conqueror of thy foes, shake off this petty-heartedness and arise (to offer battle).

The Lord knows that Arjuna's confusion was temporary as his training and his birth was of the highest. At this sad moment Arjuna was controlled by the forces of creation (Prakriti) and circumstances. This world and the after world cannot be obtained by the weak; strength is the origin of all good characteristics. The Gods and Goddesses carry weapons in their hands, symbols of strength.

2-11   *sri bhagavāna uvāca*
                       ashocyān anyashocas tvam
                       prajnāvadāms ca bhāshase
                       gatāsun agatāsums ca
                       nā 'nushocanti panditāh

The Blessed Lord said:Thou grievest for those who do not deserve to be grieved over, yet thou speaketh like a wise man. But those who are really wise grieveth neither for the dead nor for the living.

A pundit is one who knows the plan and purpose of the universe. He knows that death and rebirth are parts of this great plan just as it is usual for the Sun to set and rise. At the commencement of the Mahabharata, Arjuna forgot the great plan in the midst of his suffering. The Lord's purpose was to bring him out of this lapse of courage. Dronacharya and Bhishma understood the plan of the universe. They were ready to do battle, although because of principles, they were fighting on the opposite side of the Lord. Bhishma eventually by a display of fearlessness told Arjuna how he could be slain. The Lord asked Arjuna to harmonize his thoughts, words and deeds as he was thinking one way, speaking in another and acting in yet another. His personality was splitting. Sri Krishna was preventing this.

2-12   *na tvevāham jātu nā 'sam*
                       na tvam ne 'me janādhipāh
                       na cai 'va na bhavishyāmah
                       sarve vayam atah param

Nor I, nor you, nor any of these ruling princes was ever non-existent before; nor is it that we shall cease to be in the future.

4-5   *sri bhagavān uvāca*
                       bahuni me vyatitani
                       janmāni tava cā 'rjuna
                       tāny aham veda sarvāni
                       na tvam vettha paramtapa

The Blessed Lord said:O Arjuna, both thou and I have passed through many a life, I know all of them, thou dost not, O Chastiser of thy Foe (Arjuna).

Here the difference between an incarnation and the Jivatman comes into play. An incarnation is the manifestation of the cosmic consciousness whereas the Jivatma is a soul that is smeared by the karma on the path to cosmic consciousness. Krishna Bhagawan being sat-chid-anand knows the past, present and future. Arjuna is dealing with his senses and reacting with the circumstances around him.

4-11   **ye yathā mām prapadyante**
            tāms tathi 'va bhajāmy aham
            mama vartmā 'nuvartante
            manushyāh pārtha sarvasah

In whatever way men worship me, I favor them in the very way they seek me. O Partha, men in all ways follow my path.

The Lord understands the urge in every heart, and individually helps each to perfection. What is not good for one may be the best for the other. The ideal is to let everyone workout his/her salvation and not to have the individual confirm to another's likes or dislikes. All of us are extensions of the Lord and rest on Him.

5-29   **bhoktāram yajnatapasām**
            sarvalokamaheshvaram
            suhridam sarvabhutānām
            jnātvā mām shāntim ricchati

Having known me as the partaker of sacrifices and spiritual strivings, the Sovereign Lord of the worlds and the Friend of all creatures, he (the sage) attains peace.

It is only though the grace of the Lord and performance of Yoga we can go to liberation. God in turn grants wisdom and the appropriate fruits of our actions. Just thinking of His greatness gives one peace.

7-21   **yo-yo yām-yām tanum bhaktah**
            sraddhayā 'rcitum icchati
            tasyā-tasyā 'calām sraddhām
            tām eva vidadhāmy aham

Whatever celestial form a devotee seeks to worship with reverence, I appear to him in that form.

Worship of God as one perceives Him is not harmful as this keeps the devotee God minded. However, it is only a stepping-stone that will eventually lead to the supreme God.

10-6   ***maharsayah sapta purve***
                         catvāro manavas tathā
                         madbhāvā mānasā jātā
                         yesām loka imāh prajāh

The seven great Rishis and the four ancient Manus, endowed with My power, were born of My mind; and from them have come forth all the creatures in the world.

17-4   ***yajante sāttvikā devān***
                         yaksharakshāmsi rājasāh
                         pretān bhutaganams cā'nye
                         yajante tāmasā janāh

Men of sattvika temperament worship Gods, those of rajasic temperament worship demigods and demons and the tamasic temperament hordes of spirits and ghosts.

"Show me your company and I will tell you who you are". Good people worship the Lord in the form of Shiva, Ganesh, etc. The passionate worships the deities that is of his own temperament e.g. full of revenge or anger while, the lazy worship the Gods that tease and hurt people.

17-14   ***deva dvija guru prājna***
                         pujanam saucam ārjavam
                         brahmacaryam ahimsā ca
                         shāriram tapa ucyate

Reverence for the Gods, Brahmins, preceptors and the wise, purity, uprightness, continence and non-violence - these are the virtues, the practice of which is called the austerity of the body.

The teachers are they who set an example of spiritual life through their personal careers. They have re-cast the moulds of their lives through austerity. They have elevated themselves by getting rid of base habits of the body, mind and speech. The aspirant worshipping these great souls, get himself re-caste in the divine mould. Uprightness is to execute all bodily activities in a clean, open and

ethical way. When the thoughts, words and deeds are removed from sense and
sex pleasures and are made to only serve God, it is called continence.

7-16   *caturvidhā bhahante mām*
                                    janāh sukritino 'rjuna
                                    arto jijnāsur arthārthi
                                    jnāni ca bharatarshabha

O Best of Bharatas (Arjuna), the virtuous who worship me belong to four
types - distressed ones, knowledge-seekers, wealth-seekers and wise ones.

When Draupadi was about to be de-robed in the presence of so many, she called
on Sri Krishna and the Lord relieved of her distress.

When Swami Vivekananda relentlessly sought knowledge, the Lord gave. Only
a few seek spiritual knowledge and they receive it.

Wealth comes easily to the religious-minded. The Lord provides it without
hesitation.

The jnani through the help of the Lord can perceive through intuition,
that Brahman is the reality while the universe and the beings are all mere
superimpositions on it. Adoring Brahman is his worship.

These four types of worshippers are virtuous because of their right
understanding.
7-17   *teshām jnāni nityayukta*
                                    ekabhaktir vishishyate
                                    priyo hi jnānino 'tyartham
                                    aham sa ca mama priyah

Among them, the wise one who is ever centered in the Divine, given to
single-minded devotion, is the highest. For I am exceedingly dear to him
and he to Me.

The Jnani is dearer to the Lord because he sees himself as one with God and
creation.

7-20   *kāmais tais tair hritajnānāh*
                                    prapadyante 'nyadevatāh
                                    tam-tam niyamam āsthāya
                                    prakrityā niyatāh svayā

Men whose reason has been led astray by worldly desires, worship other Gods being bound by their own nature, resort to various rites.

Once Swami Pranavanandaji was asked by one of His monk disciples as to why he was not using His spiritual powers to create food as they were starving. His reply was that "Why should I prostitute my power for such a trifling thing when food could be obtained by mere begging, and by the duty of a monk". He continued to say, that why ask for small insignificant things when through sacrifice the monk disciple can receive liberation. Here Lord Krishna was saying why not surrender to Him instead of asking for worldly comforts.

9-18   **gatir bhartā prabhuh sākshi**
                nivāshah sharanam suhrit
                prabhavah pralayah sthānam
                nidhānam bijam avyayam

I am the Goal, Supporter, Lord, Witness, the Abode, Refuge, Friend, Beginning and End, Resting place, Store-house and the Eternal seed.

The goal of all people can be sorted in the three classes -

    i)   Striving for long efficient life.
    ii) Seeking for wider knowledge
    iii) Searching for more happiness and glorification from the masses.

These are the modifications of Sat-chid-anand, Life, light and love and are the definitions of God.

9-25   **yānti devavratā davān**
                pitrin yānti bhutejyā
                bhutani yanti bhutejya
                yānti madyājino 'pi mām

Worshippers of the Gods go to the Gods, ancestor-worshippers go to the manes, worshippers of the spirits go to the spirits and My worshippers come unto Me.

Worship of deities brings one closer to the supreme God but deities also are subject to rebirth. One may get long life or supernatural powers from worship of deities but these are hindrances to devotion, knowledge and liberation.

Worship of ancestors is beneficial for elevation of their souls but attachment or worship (priest craft) of ancestors has no value for the aspirant instead it is harmful for spiritual life.

Bhutas (between Devas and man) worship leads to psychic powers and bondage. The yogi is he who bypasses all these trivial worships and seeks to surrender himself to the Lord.

9-26
**patram pushpam phalam toyam
yo me bhaktyā prajacchati
tad aham bhaktyupahritam
ashnāmi prayatātmanah**

Whatever man gives Me in true devotion whether a leaf, a flower, a fruit or water, I accept that gift of love from the pure soul.

Here bhakti devotion is the key as we have seen with the example of Sabari offering dry fruits to Sri Rama, Sudama offering puffed rice to Sri Krishna and Vidur offering gruel to the Lord. All in turn received great rewards.

9-27
**yat karoshi yad ashnāsi
yaj juhosi dadāsi yat
yat tapasyasi kaunteya
tat kurusva madarpanam**

O Son of Kunti (Arjuna), whatever thou does, eatest or giveth, whatever thou offerest as sacrifice and whatever austerities thou performest, do that as an offering unto Me.

Sri Ramakrishna usually prayed to Mother Kali "My doings are all your doings, not I, not I but you". At Bharat Sevashram Sangha surrender, detachment and celibacy is a necessity for spiritual progress. These are all aids to better dedicate one's life to serving society. However, serving society and these austerities are just means to self-realization and not the goal.

9-31
**kshipram bhavati dharmātmā
shashvacchāntim nigacchati
kaunteya pratijānihi
na me bhaktah pranashyati**

This depraved person soon turns into a virtuous one and gains eternal peace. O Son of Kunti (Arjuna), you can safely swear that My devotee never comes to grief.

Faith in the Lord is an indispensable ingredient. It is best to lose all worldly belongings including relationships but faith in God must be maintained. The Pandavas lost their kingdom, their lives were in constant jeopardy, they were taunted and belittled, but in the end they got salvation.

10-14
> ***sarvam etad ritam manye***
> ***yan mām vadasi keshava***
> ***na hi te bhagavan vyaktim***
> ***vidur devā na dānavāh***

O Keshava, I believe as true all that thou tellest the Gods; neither the demons, O Lord, nor I know Thy manifestations.

The following six qualities are fully manifested only in the Lord - omnipotence, dharma-righteousness, aishvarya-Lordship, Sri-wealth and beauty, jnana-knowledge/wisdom, vairagya-dispassion. He is also knower of past, present and future. The Demigods cannot come close to these features.

10-22
> ***vedānām sāmvedo 'smi***
> ***devānām asmi vāsavah***
> ***indriyānām manas cā 'smi***
> ***bhutānām asmi cetanā***

Among the Vedas, I am the Samveda; among the Gods, I am Indra; among the senses, I am the mind; and I am consciousness in living beings.

Samveda is musical and thus enjoyed by all. Indra has risen to perfection and was thus awarded the position of Lord of the Devas. Mind records the information fed by the senses. Pure consciousness is another name for the original God.

10-23
> ***rudrānām samkaras cāsmi***
> ***vittesho yaksha-rakshasām***
> ***vasunām pāvakas cāsmi***
> ***meruh shikharinām aham***

Among the Rudras (the eleven Gods of destruction), I am Sankara (Siva); among the Yakshas and Rakshashas, the God of wealth (Kuvera). Among the Vasus, I am the God of fire (Agni) and among the mountain-peaks I am Meru.

The Rudras are eleven in number and their function is to cry and crave for eternal happiness (Sreyas). Lord Sankara through struggle takes the spiritual aspirant quickly to the purified state.

Wealth wields power, a glory of God. Yakshas are specialists in acquiring wealth and the Rakshas are good at hoarding it. Kuvera is the king of these two categories. Vasus are eight in number, the five elements, sun, moon and stars. Of them fire is most essential and is referred to as His special manifestation. Mount Meru is compared to the axis of heavily bodies and also the spinal cords of humans. God gives it its brilliance.

10-24   *purodhasām ca mukhyam mām*
            viddhi pārtha brihaspatim
            senāninām aham skandah
            sarasām asmi sāgarah

O Partha, among priests, knows Me to be their chief, Brihaspati; among the generals, I am Skanda (Kartikeya); and among the waters I am the ocean.

Brihaspati is the king of rituals and one prays to him for wisdom and learning. Skanda or Kartikeya, the son of Lord Shiva is best at warfare. The ocean is the symbol of vastness. The Lord is all of this.

10-26   *ashvatthah sarvavrikshānām*
            devarshinām ca nāradah
            gandharvānām citrarathah
            siddhānām kapilo munih

Among trees, I am the Asvattha (the holy fig or peepul tree) and Narada among the celestial sages. I am Chitraratha among the celestial singers (Gandharvas) and the sage Kapila among the Siddhas (perfected ones).

Asvattha or fig tree has no useful fruit to man but it creates a presence of God. Narada is an enlightened soul and foremost among the enlightened souls or

Rishis. He is noted for always chanting "Narayana" and starting off quarrels which are blessings in disguise. He is God in disguise.

The Gandharvas are heavenly bodies that are expert physicians and musicians, gamblers, very lustful, knower of the Vedas and sometimes play the role of teachers to the Rishis. Chitraratha is their king.

Sage Kapila like all other munis is constantly engaged in japa. He is born, righteous and wise, and possesses dispassion. The Lord claims him, as His own as he is an incarnation of Vishnu.

10-28
**āyudhānām aham vajram
dhenunām asmi kāmadhuk
prajanas cā 'smi kandarpah
sarpānām asmi vāsukih**

Among weapons, I am the thunderbolt; among cows, I am the celestial cow, Kamadhuk and of the progenitors, I am Kandarpa (the God of love) and Vasuki among serpents.

The vajra or thunderbolt was made from the bone of the sage Dadhichi upon the request of Lord Indra. It represents the sacrifice of holy men and women for public welfare. An exuberant mind and wholesome ventures are the glories of God. Sage Vasistha received everything because of his possession of Kamadhuk, a cow that was a product from the churning of the ocean.

The venomous serpent, Vasuki is symbolic of the cosmic energy and the pairs of opposites. In man, it is the dominant kundalini or serpent power. It was wrapped around mount Meru when the ocean was churned for the nectar of youthful life.

11-8
**na tu mām shakyase drashtum
anenai 'va svacakshusha
divyam dadāmi te cakshuh
pashya me yogam aishvaram**

But thou canst not behold Me with these eyes of yours. I give to Thee the divine vision. Behold My marvelous power.

Man with all his progressive mastery over the knowledge of nature has not solved the problems of life and death. Spiritual life fills this void or mystery.

Through the grace of God, the spiritual aspirant merges his personal will with that of the cosmic will, thereby becoming a God realized soul. Intuition or the third eye is the fruit of this union. God realization in the various planes of the consciousness -

Mental plain - *the phenomenon*
Ethical plain - *infallible law*
Divine eye level - *kinetic or active God*
Intuitive level - *static God*

After these levels, the individuals merge with God. Arjuna was bestowed by Lord's grace with the divine eye and so all his problems disappeared.

16-5   ***daivi sampad vimokshāya***
              nibandhāyāsuri matā
              mā shucah sampadam daivim
              abhijāto 'si pāndava

Divine properties lead to liberation and the demoniac to bondage. Grieve not, O Pandava, for thou art born with divine heritage.

The Lord, the knower of past and present assured Arjuna that he is of divine birth and was well on his path to liberation. Man accrues the good and bad birth after birth. The demonical perpetuates this cycle whereas in the case of Arjuna, God realization was getting closer.

18-61   ***ishvarah sarvabhutānām***
              hriddeshe'rjuna tishthati
              bhrāmayan sarvabhutani
              yantrārudhāni māyayā

The Lord resides in the heart of all beings, O Arjuna and turns them round and round, as if mounted on a machine, by His Maya (illusive power).

The Lord resides in the heart as a witness and His presence prompts beings to duty. The word Arjuna means white in colour and pure in nature and so he was entitled to know the truth. God through Maya causes His creation to be ever active in a systematic way leading towards universal perfection. He is a true spiritual aspirant who knows he is not the doer but just an instrument in the hands of the Lord. The ignorant thinks that by crooked manipulation, they can cause things to happen.

18-65   *manmanā bhava madbhakto*
                   madyāji mām namaskuru
                   mamevai'shyasi satyam te
                   pratijāne priyo'si me

Become My-minded, My lover and adorer, a sacrificer to Me, bow thyself
to Me and thou shalt come; this is My pledge and promise to thee, for
dear art thou to Me.

The purpose of Sri Krishna's incarnation is to say the truth of His relationship
with the embodied soul (Jivatman). Just like the sun can only radiate its rays.
The various schools of thoughts discuss the relationship of the individual souls
with the cosmic soul and in the end the realization that these two are the same
is the goal of life.

It is the nature of the mind to seek pleasant and enjoyable things that are
countered non-productive towards self-realization. When the love for God
overshadows love for worldly possessions then the Lord is obligated to reciprocate
likewise (Bhakta Prahlad).

18-67   *idam te nā 'tapaskāya*
                   nā 'bhaktāya kadācana
                   na cāshushrushave vācyam
                   na ca mām yo 'bhyasuyati

Never speak of this to anyone who does not lead an austere life, who is
lacking in devotion and is unwilling to hear nor to one who bears malice
towards Me.

The Lord is saying here that Bhagavad-Gita will not benefit people whose lives
are without discipline and austerity. Life without austerity is incomplete for
spiritual progress, to them, the Gita is of no benefit. If someone is not interested
in the Gita, then it should not be preached to him.

18-69   *na ca tasmān manushyeshu*
                   kashcin me priyakrittamah
                   bhavitā na ca me tasmād
                   anyah priyataro bhuvi

There is none among men who can do Me a dearer service than this nor can there be one on earth dearer to Me (Nor shall any one else be dearer to Me on earth).

Gita explains the workings of the universe and the laws governing human life. Knowledge of the divine and mundane is adequately explained. Prosperity in earthly life and attainment of Godhood are expounded. It is the summary of all scriptures, and therefore if it is expounded to spiritual aspirants. It expounds the path to universal emancipation also. The Lord is saying that this is the highest service that one can perform as an instrument in His hands.

18-70   ***adhyeshyate ca ya imam***
dharmyamsamvādamāvayoh
jnānayajnena tenāham
ishtah syāmiti me matih

And if any man studies this sacred discourse of ours, I shall consider that he worships Me through the yajna of knowledge.

Reading and practicing Gita is one of the highest forms of worship of the Lord. The more we know of the workings of God, the more we will adore and worship Him, and this is the purpose of life. His drama is so vast and endless. It is the alternative to useless mundane thinking, speaking and mundane actions.

18-71   ***shraddhāvān anasuyash ca***
shrinuyād api yo narah
so'pi muktah shubhāmllokān
prāpnuyāt punyakarmanām

If a man simply listens to it with faith and without malice, he, too, will be freed from his sins and repair to the heaven of the righteous.

Being an expert at academic explanation and not following it has no spiritual value. However the person who listens to it and follows even a little, will reap the appropriate fruit. The essence of religion lies in its practice and realization.

"Spirituality is not something to be gained by scriptural studies and hearsay. Mad indeed is the one who thinks of unravelling the mysteries of spiritual life with the help of a mind torn by passions, tyrannized by the senses and agonized by carnal hankerings"Swami Pranavananda.

18-72   *kaccid etac chrutam pārtha*
                   tvayai'kāgrena cetasā
                   kaccid ajnānasammohah
                   pranashtaste dhananjaya

O Partha (Arjuna), have thou listened to this with rapt attention? O Winner of Wealth (Arjuna), hast thy delusion arising out of ignorance been dispelled?

Concentration is the key to proper understanding; a concentrated mind can lead to an enlightened soul, whereas a destructive mind keeps one in ignorance. Ignorance and knowledge cannot coexist. Sri Krishna wanted to find out whether Arjuna's hesitation to do righteous battle with the revered ones has been overcome.

God as creation

ELEMENTS AND NATURE

3-5
na hi kascit kshanam api
jātu tisthaty akarmakrit
kāryate hy avashah karma
sarvah prakritijair gunaih

Nobody can even take a moment off without doing work; for everybody is impelled to act in spite of himself by natural impulses.

Creation in its entirety is kinetic energy or moving energy. From the tiny atom to the vast universe, there are ceaseless actions caused by the gunas. It is a misconception that one can cease from action. Breathing, sleeping, beating of the heart etc., are continuous actions or karma. Until we master good action we are students of nature. When we do master it we fuse into Brahman or the action less plane.

3-27
prakriteh kriyamānāni
gunaih karmāni sarvashah
ahamkāravimudhātmā
kartā 'ham iti manyate

All the work is carried out by the different modes of nature. The fool deluded by egoism fancies himself to be the sole doer.

When the embodied being ignores the presence of the perfected soul, then the intellect, mind and senses become the ruling factor over the body. They react to a changing environment and according to their evolutions and the presence of the inherent forces of the gunas. In the absence of the perfected soul they claim doer ship. This is egoism. However, if the soul is sought for guidance through meditation, then these become its slave and are accordingly guided to right action. Here the soul being the observer also becomes the guide, as it is a ray of the perfected self. Egoism vanishes for in reality it is a nonentity.

3-29   *prakriter gunasammudhāh*
                        sajjante gunakarmasu
                      tān akritsnavido mandān
                      kritsnavin na vicālayet

Those who come under the spell of prakriti become attached to the actions
flowing from gunas. He who knows every thing should not distract the
minds of those little-knowing dullards.

*Individuals who cannot differentiate between nature and soul should be left to
perform their allotted duties and always be active. They will eventually evolve
into the state of Godhood.*

4-6   *ajo 'pi sann avyayātmā*
                        bhutānām isvaro 'pi san
                     prakritim svām adhisthāya
                     sambhavāmy ātmamāyayā

I am not bound by the cycles of birth, and am immortal and Lord of
all beings. Yet remaining steadfast in my own nature, I come into being
through my own divine power (Maya, mysterious power).

*The play of nature or creation is a stage for both God and man. Lord Krishna
controlled her (Prakriti) actions while Arjuna is a slave to Maya Sakti (illusion).
The same way the Lord creates the universe in the same manner as He manifests
Himself. God has nothing to gain as He is the architect and assumes forms to
be a role model.*

7-4   *bhumir āpo 'nalo vāyuh*
                     kham mano buddhir eva ca
                       ahamkāra iti 'yam me
                     bhinnā prakritir ashtadhā

Earth, water, fire, air, ether, mind, reason and ego – these comprise of My
eightfold divided nature.

The five elements have their corresponding sense organs and senses.

Ear *perceives sounds using the element ether.*
Skin *perceives touch using the element air.*
Eye *perceives form using the elements of light and fire.*
Tongue *perceives taste using the element water and*
Nose *perceives smell using the element earth.*

The mind is the combination of all the senses and produces a feeling. The intellect interprets the feeling and decides what are good or bad actions and egoism claims doer-ship.

7-5
**apare 'yam itas tv anyām
prakritim viddhi me parām
jivabhutām mahābāho
yaye 'dam dhāryate jagat**

O Mighty-armed One (Arjuna), this is my inferior (insentient) Nature and distinct from it, you should understand, is my other Nature in the form of life-consciousness, which sustains this world.

The five senses, mind, intellect and ego form the inferior aspect of the Lord. The sum total of the individual souls forms His superior aspect. The Jivatmans are mere sparks of the Cosmic Soul or Paramatman and they are not separate from it, just as the waves are not a separate entity from the ocean.

9-7
**sarvabhutāni kaunteya
prakritim yanti māmikām
kalpakshaye punastāni
kalpādau visrijāmyaham**

O Son of Kunti (Arjuna), at the end of every kalpa (cycle) all beings go back to My prakriti (nature) and at the beginning of the next kalpa, I create them anew.

At the end of one day (incalculable number of years) of Brahma, all the manifested goes into the un-manifested and remains dormant for equal number of years, (a night for Brahman). Day and night of Brahman are part of a continuous process.

9-8
**prakritim svām avastabhya
visrijāmi punah punah
bhutagrāmam imam krisnam
avasham prakriter vashāt**

Taking control of my own prakriti (nature), I create again and again the entire mass of these beings, who are helpless beings swayed by their own prakriti (nature).

The presence of Isvara causes nature to act, thereby animating it but Isvara is unconcerned and unattached to the actions of Prakriti.

9-10   **mayā 'dhyaksena prakritih**
                 suyate sacarācaram
                 hetunā 'nena kaunteya
                 jagad viparivartate

It is under My lead that Nature (prakriti) brings forth all things, both animate and inanimate, and because of this, O Son of Kunti (Arjuna), the world goes revolving.

First the Lord creates everything that is manifested out of Himself. Secondly, the whole of creation becomes an instrument of his will by being animated by him. Thirdly he detaches himself and stays in the background. In the same way, the rays of the Sun are beneficial while the sun remains in the background. The Lord is called Adhyaksha as he provides and keeps an alert eye on the total efficiency of the functioning of His creation.

10-29   **anantas cā 'smi nāgānām**
                 varuno yādasām aham
                 pitrinām aryamā cā 'smi
                 yamah samyamatām aham

Among nagas, I am Ananta; among beings having their abode in the waters, I am Varuna; among the ancestros, I am Aryama. And among those responsible for maintenance of discipline, I am Yama.

Ananta *of the nonpoisonous snakes represents the five elements as it has five heads.*

Varuna *is the Lord of water.*

Aryama *was the first to enter the world of the departed ancestors and became the Lord.*

Yama *is the king of self-control. He does not deviate an iota on the Day of Judgment and punishment. The above are the qualities of God.*

13-3   *ksetrajnam cā 'pi mām viddhi*
              sarva ksetresu bhārata
              ksetra ksetrajnayor jnānam
              yat taj jnānam matam mama

And know from Me as to the Kshetrajna (Consciousness) in all Kshetras (Universe). The Knowledge of both is deemed by me as true knowledge.

God through the elements established the material universe. With His life force the universe was animated. The life force is referred to as Jivatmans. To know the workings of creation is lower knowledge (apara vidya) or academic learning while knowledge of life force is higher knowledge (para vidya) or direct experience. Both these types of knowledge are important for life's fulfillment.

Once Lord Shiva put a test to His two sons Ganesh and Kartikeya. They were asked to circle the universe and the one that won would receive a celestial gift. Ganesh after deliberation moved around Lord Shiva and Mother Parbati and claimed the prize while His brother sped off on his peacock. Modern day man is like Kartikeya. We spend much time making discoveries of the material world which is but a stepping stone to knowledge of the spirit.

13-5   *rsibhir bahudhā gitam*
              chandobhir vividaih prthak
              brahmasutrapadais cai 'va
              hetumadbhir viniscitaih

This has been sung by Rishis in many ways, in various distinctive chants, in passages indicative of Brahman, full of reasoning and conviction.

This knowledge was recorded in script and music by the Rishis. Sage Narada is the prime example as he conveyed his message with chanting and a combination of intellect and love. Music that creates sentiment only is harmful for it can arouse the animalistic behavior in man.

13- 20   *prakritim purusham cai 'va*
              viddhy anādi ubhāv 'api
              vikārāms ca gunāms cai 'va
              viddhi prakritisambhavān

Know thou that both Purusha (soul) and Prakriti (nature) are without a beginning. Know this also that the gunas and all modifications are born of Prakriti.

As the ocean is sometimes still and sometimes furious, so Purusha is action less while nature is ever changing, as it is the embodiment of time, space and causation. Although Nature, (Prakriti) seems to be separate from God, it has no beginning and no end. The Lord said He is both.

13-21   ***kārya-kārana kartritve
                          hetuh prakritir ucyate
                          purusha sukhaduhkhānām
                          bhoktritve hetur ucyate***

Prakriti (nature) is said to be the source of cause and effect, while Purusha (soul) is the cause of experiencing pleasure and pain.

The five elements make up the human body and nature. God as the supreme is called Purusha. His creation is just an inferior aspect of himself, just as a son is to the father. The senses of perception and actions service the Jivatma. The Jivatma or soul experiences pain and pleasure from birth to birth. It gets trained to separate the real from unreal. Upon doing so, it frees itself and joins the unchangeable supreme Self. It becomes free from Prakriti (creation).

13-22   ***purushah prakritistho hi
                          bhunkte prakritijān gunāh
                          kāranam gunasango 'sya
                          sadasadyonijanmasu***

Purusha, being identified with Prakriti, enjoys the modes born of it. His attachment to them is the cause of good or evil birth.

The individual souls are educated by the gunas based on the sensations fed by the sense organs. If it adheres to goodness (sattvika) it eventually evolves to perfection or liberation. If it adheres to passion (tamasika) it is born as a lower creature and if it adheres to a mixture, it is born as a mundane man.

13-24   ***ya evam vetti purusham
                          prakritim ca gunaih saha
                          sarvathā vartamāno 'pi
                          na sa bhuyo 'bhijāyate***

He who thus knows Purusha and Prakriti together with the gunas (modes), no matter what his mode of life is, is not born again.

Knowledge of the oneness of the self (Atma) and nature makes one fit for self-realization. Once he has this realization, the bondage of current karmas (actions, words and thoughts) has no effect on him. He is only burning out past karmas and this is what is keeping the body going. When all the past and current residue of karmas are burnt away, the need for a mundane body stops. The unreal is realized and only the pure consciousness exists. The Jivatma becomes the supreme soul.

13-30
  prakrityai 'va ca karmāni
  kriyamānāni sarvashah
  yah pashyati tathātmānam
  akartāram sa pashyati

He who sees that all actions are done by Prakriti (nature) and that the self is not the doer, sees truly.

The Jnani, more than anyone else is full of activities because of his duty to set the perfect example. However, he knows his true identity is action less . No person can stay action less so long as he is in the body. We have to admire God in his action less state and also in His ever- active manifested state.

14-3
  mama yonir mahad brahma
  tasmin garbham dadhāmy aham
  sambhavah sarvabhutānām
  tato bhavati bhārata

My womb is the Mahat Brahma (the whole of nature) and in that I place the germ. Thence, O Bharata, is the birth of all beings.

The lord is called all pervasive because he manifests a small fraction of Himself to manifested creation. Matter and spirit come together to create the universe just like a father and mother

14-4
  sarvayonishu kaunteya
  murtayah sambhavanti yāh
  tāsām brahma mahad yonir
  aham bijapradah pitā

O Son of Kunti (Arjuna), whatever forms are born of wombs, great Prakriti is the womb and I am the father who plants the seed.

Functions of the gunas (5-12)

14-5
sattvam rajas tama iti
gurāh prakritisambhavāh
nibadhnanti mahābāho
dehe dehinam avyayam

O Mighty-armed (Arjuna), the three modes (gunas) sattva (goodness), rajas (passion), tamas (dullness, ignorance), born of Prakriti, bind the immutable soul in the body.

In Prakriti are the three modes (gunas). These modes of nature are the active rays of the creator, God, and as such have no effect on Him. The ceaseless actions of the gunas on the embodied souls cause the individuals to experience variety and modification in the same way as the ripples in water cause the Sun to appear trembling. The soul is always the same.

14-6
tatra sattvam nirmalatvāt
prakāshakam anāmayam
sukhasangena badhnāti
jnānasangena canagha

O Sinless One (Arjuna), of these sattva being pure is luminous and free from evil. It binds the soul nonetheless in as much as it leads to a search for happiness (joy) and a longing for knowledge.

A disciple of sattvika qualities radiates the brilliance of the soul. However, secular knowledge (the art of seeing creation in it apparent sense) and sacred knowledge (the intuitive faculty of seeing God as consciousness) go hand in hand. Pleasure is derived from both so the aspirant gets attached. This causes bondage and therefore a hindrance for God realization.

14-7
rajo rāgātmakam viddhi
trishnāsangasamudbhavam
tannibadhnāti kaunteya
karmasangena dehinam

O Son of Kunti (Arjuna), know rajas to be of the nature of passion from which springs desire and attachment. It binds the embodied self by attachment to action.

14-8
    tamas tv ajnānajam viddhi
    mohanam sarvadehinām
    pramādālasya nidrābhis tan
    nibadhnāti bhārata

But know Tamas to be born of ignorance, deluding all embodied beings; it binds fast, Arjuna, by heedlessness, indolence and sleep.

14-9
    sattvam sukhe sanjayati
    rajah karmani bhārata
    jnānam āvritya tu tamah
    pramāde sanjayaty uta

O Bharata (Arjuna), sattva links the soul to happiness and rajas to action, but tamas, veiling wisdom, leads to heedlessness (negligence).

14-11
    sarvadvareshu dehe 'smin
    prakāsha upajāyate
    jnānam yadā tadā vidyād
    vivriddham sattvam ity uta

When knowledge emerges as light through all the sense-openings in the body, then know that sattva is in the ascendant.

When the thought is right then actions radiate brilliance. The eyes become sharp, ears alert, speech commanding etc.

14-12
    lobhah pravrittir ārambhah
    karmanām ashamah spril ā
    rajasyetani jāyante
    vivriddhe bharatarshabha

Greed, activity, enterprise, restlessness, longing (desire) - these prevail, O Best of Bhāratas (Arjuna), when rajas is predominant.*Qualities of Rajas: -*
 Desires - *goading to start new projects*
 Trishna - *craving to acquire new items*
 Sanga - *clinging on to acquired objects.*

Greed - *craving to do or acquire another's property or idea*
Doing the work that belongs to another
Doing too much leading to elation or doing too little leading to a
feeling of failure or dejection.
Longing - *to have something done immediately without planning*
Unrest - *mind always moving at high speed*

These qualities prompt individual souls to think they themselves are the agents
of action. (14-7 & 12)

15-7   *mamai 'vā 'msho jivaloke*
jivabhutah sanātanah
manahshashthāni 'ndriyāni
prakritisthāni karshati

A portion of Myself becomes an eternal soul in the world of life and draws
to itself the senses of which the mind is the sixth. All abide in Prakriti.

The title Jivatma connotes that the aspirant is bound and controlled by the
gunas and through this ignorance the five senses and the mind are born. His
existence, he feels is to properly react to the environment and to the external
world. This feeling causes bondage to the sensual pleasures, therefore repeated
births. The Jivatma is never given a chance to be the controlling factor; it only
remains as the witness. The covering shell that the gunas have formed over the
Atma has to be cracked and broken to pieces and then the individual self is
revealed.

The gunas and happiness (36-39)

18-36   *sukham tv idānim trividham*
shrinu me bharatarshabha
abhyāsād ramate yatra
dukhāntam ca nigacchati

And now hear from me, Arjuna, of the three kinds of happiness, in which
a man comes to rejoice by long practice and by which he reaches the end
of his sorrow.

All beings are relentlessly exerting themselves in the quest for happiness. This drive
is motivated by nature or gunas, and is endless. The enlightened ones have received
this everlasting happiness but the masses are spending their life searching for it.

18-37
yat tad agre visam iva
parināme mrtopamam
tat sukham sāttvikam proktam
ātma buddhi prasādajam

That which is like poison at first, but like nectar at the end; that happiness is said to be Sattvika, born of the translucence of intellect due to self-realization.

When a man becomes a slave to lust, he falls and becomes a slave to man also, losing his happiness thereby. Birth after birth the soul has got accustomed to life in the body. His going back to free spiritual life is a painful, new endeavor. But upon realizing that his true self is beyond time, space and causation he feels like a fish back in water. For the sattvika person this seems insurmountable in the beginning but like honey in the end.

18-38
visayendriyasamyogad
yat tad agre 'mrtopamam
parināme visam iva tat
sukham rājasam smritam

That happiness which arises from the contact of the senses and their objects is like nectar at first but like poison at the end – it is held to be Rajasika.

Happiness obtained from the contact of the senses eventually robs one of his stamina. This eventually leads to untold misery like senility, lack of concentration. Thereby he cannot hold a job and resorts to adharma to maintain life

The fruits received from the churning of the ocean was poison and nectar of everlasting youthful life. In addition came out figures which were symbolic of the niceties of life. But immediately came the fear of death caused by chasing after the nectar. What was perceived as happiness ended as war between the righteous and the unrighteous. Following the sattvika life and surrendering to the ever immortal Lord Shiva all the poisons of life will be removed.

18-39
yad agre cā 'nubandhe ca
sukham mohanam ātmanah
nidrālasya pramādottham
tat tāmasam udāhritam

That happiness which deludes the self both at the beginning and at the end and which arises from sleep, sloth and miscomprehension -that is declared to be Tamasika.

Happiness that is obtained from the consumption of intoxicating drinks causes drowning of the senses. This results in depression, loss of respect from society and misery in the household. Sleep is necessary but at the call of duty it should be a means for the revitalizing of the body and mind and not for pleasure.

18-40
    na tad asti prithivyām vā
    divi deveshu vā punah
    sttavam prakritijair muktam
    yadebhih syāt tribhir gunaih

There is no creature on earth or in heaven among the Gods, which is free from the influence of the three gunas arising from nature (Prakriti).

All created beings including Brahma, the creator, are bound by the kinetic energy, the gunas. Brahma is not a liberated soul but is the highest of the embodied souls or Jivatmans. He is going through his final reincarnation. It is through these active forces or gunas he can create. At the end of his day (kalpa), he will gain gradually liberation or go beyond the gunas.

God as creation

EXCELLENCE IN NATURE

7-8
raso 'ham apsu kaunteya
prabhā 'smi shashisuryayoh
pranavah sarvavedeshu
shabdah khe paurusham nrishu

O Kaunteya (Arjuna), I am the taste in water. I am the light in the moon and the sun. I am sacred Om in all the Vedas. I am the sound in ether and prowess in men.

Isvara should be recognized in all of His manifestations. Pure water is tasteless but the power of God in it adds taste. Colour, form and beauty of Fire, Sun and Moon are realized when perceived by the eye. Ether is the vehicle of sound of which OM contains all the possible sounds and specific sounds become language. The five elements correspond to the five senses and form the base of knowledge of nature. Through the excellence of God man fulfills his existence and so gains contentment or manliness.

7-9
punyo gandhah prithivyām ca
tejas cā 'smi vibhāvasau
jivanam sarvabhuteshu
tapas cā 'smi tapasvishu

I am the sacred fragrance in earth and radiance in fire. I am the life in all beings and austerity in ascetics.

Fire and sun is a reminder of the ever lasting splendor of the Lord. Meditation on them sparks the everlasting bliss of the soul in man, and eventually leads to freedom from death. Austerity is the act of intensifying one's life to achieve self-realization. The Lord is famous for sanctions and grants. The Lord is famous for His severe austerity and so has been given the name Ghora Tapasvin.

7-10
bijam mām sarvabhutānām
viddhi pārtha sanātanam
bhddhir buddhimatām asmi
tejas tejasvinām aham

O Partha (Arjuna), know me to be the eternal seed of all beings. I am the intellect of the intellectuals. I am the prowess of the powerful.

As the ocean is the continuous source of clouds so God is the constant source of the sustenance of His creation. Adoration of the vast variety of beings is adoration of the Lord. The study and understanding of the intelligence of the variety leads to self-realization. The Lord adores one who sees Him in His varied manifested state. Facial glow (tejas) and inner light (ojas) are the reflections of the righteous life one lives. This is a symbol of the splendor of the presence of the Lord.

7-11   ***balam balavatām asmi***
                       kāmarāgavivarjitam
                       dharmāviruddho bhuteshu
                       kāmo 'smi bharatarshabha

O Lord of the Bharatas (Arjuna), I am the prowess of the strong, purged of desire and passion. I am desire in beings, which runneth not contrary to the law or the injunctions of Dharma.

Kama (desire)-is the hankering for invisible desires not yet obtained while raga (passion) is the holding on to visible and obtained objects. Ravana by abducting Seeta wanted to make Her his own. He is a prime example. Sri Rama performing righteous duties is void of these weaknesses. Not all desires are vices ex: the desire to excel another in good conduct and the craving to obtain the grace of God.

The fly will sit on clean food and then sits on filth but the bee will only suck the honey from the flowers and then go straight to the hive. The aspirants are like the fly and the bee like a paramahansa.

7-12   ***ye cai 'va sāttvikā bhāvā***
                        rājasās tāmasās ca ye
                        matta eve 'ti tān viddhi
                        na tv aham teshu te mayi

Whatever states of beings there may exist, sattvika, rajas or tamas - know them to be emanating from Me alone. I am not in them.

9-6
> *yathā 'kasasthito nityam*
> *vāyuh sarvatrago mahān*
> *tathā sarvāni bhutāni*
> *matsthāni ty upadhāraya*

As the air, vast and always moving everywhere, abides in the expanse of ether, so all beings, know thou this, exist in me.

9-16
> *aham kratur aham yajnah*
> *svadhā 'ham aham aushadham*
> *mantroham aham evājyam*
> *aham agnir aham hutam*

I am the Vedic ritual, I am the sacrifice, I am the oblation to manes, I am the medicinal herb, I am the hymn, I am the sacrificial butter, I am the sacred fire and the offering.

God is everything, nothing can exist without him. Yajna is the Vedic sacrifice of giving our self to the universal self. The gift and the surrender are both His.

9-17
> *pitā 'ham asya jagato*
> *mātā dhātā pitāmahah*
> *vedyam pavitram omkāra*
> *rik sāma yajur eva ca*

I am the father of this world, the mother, the sustainer and the grandsire. I am the goal of knowledge, the purifier. I am the syllable Om and I am the Sama, Rik and Yajus Vedas as well.

10-31
> *pavanah pavatām asmi*
> *rāmah sastrabhrtām aham*
> *jhasānām makaras cā 'smi*
> *srotasām asmi jāhnavi*

Of purifiers I am the wind; of the wielders of weapon I am Rama. Of fishes I am the shark, and of rivers I am the Ganges.

10-36   *dyutam chalayatām asmi*
                       tejas tejasvinām aham
                       jayo 'smi vyavasāyo 'smi
                       sattvam sattvavatām aham

I am the gambling of the fraudulent, I am the splendor of the splendid;
I am victory; I am effort; I am the goodness of the good.

10-39   *yac cā 'pi sarvabhutānām*
                       bijam tad aham arjuna
                       na tad asti vinā yat syān
                       mayā bhutam carācaram

Further O Arjuna, I am the seed of all beings; nor is there anything
moving or inert that can exist without Me in the three worlds, O Thou
Incomparable in Might?

15-12   *yad ādityagatam tejo*
                       jagad bhāsayate 'khilam
                       yaccandramasi yaccāgnau
                       tat tejo viddhi māmakam

The radiance of the Sun that lights up the whole world, that which is found
in the moon and in fire - that radiance, know this, belongs to Me.

*The light of the Sun, Moon and Fire are the outcome of the sattva nature or the
reflection of consciousness. The visual lights are mere reflections but the light of
the cosmic self is consciousness.*

15-13   *gāmāvishya ca bhutāni*
                       dhārayāmy aham ojasā
                       pushnāmi caushadhih sarvāh
                       somo bhutvā rasātmakah

Entering the earth, I sustain all beings with my vital energy and nourish
all plants and trees. I am the Moon, which is the giver (source) of water
and sap.

*Without the Sun and Moon's energy life cannot exist on earth. Heat from the
Sun energizes the living beings and the plants use it for the manufacturing of
food. The animals and men eat the plants for energy.*

The sap in plants comes from the Moon's energy. All these forms of energy are the energy rays of God. This energy pervades the universe.

15-14   ***aham vaishvānaro bhutvā***
                      prāninām deham āshritah
                      prānāpānasamāyuktah
                      pacāmy annam caturvidham

I become the fire of life within the frame of all living beings and being linked with the ingoing and outgoing breath, I digest the four kinds of food.

Our breathing fuels body heat and gastric heat. The four elements earth, fire, water and air are the constituents of the four kinds of foods.

CHAPTER - II

How can one get into a relationship with God?

Faith

3-31
> *ye me matam idam nityam*
> *anutishthanti mānavāh*
> *shraddhavanto 'nasuyanto*
> *mucyante te 'pi karmabhih*

Those who ever abide by this teaching of Mine, full of sraddha and free from cavilling, they too are released from actions.

Faith is the state of mind conducive to all round advancement. Reading the Bhagavad Gita with the conviction that it is the instructions of God, is faith. Surrendering to the guru, placing faith in fellow human beings and applying oneself to a task is also faith.

Contrary to faith is caviling – intolerant of others and insisting his/her progress shall be recognized. Persons of this nature cannot progress in spiritual life, but the Lord washes the sins away of the meek and humble.

4-39
> *sraddhāvān labhate jnānam*
> *tatparah samyatendriyah*
> *jnānam labdhvā param shāntim*
> *acirenā 'dhigacchati*

He who has reverence and faith, is steadfast and continent, gains wisdom and having gained wisdom, he very soon achieves the supreme peace.

The quest to know God needs maximum zeal and faith. Obedience to the preceptor, through whole-hearted service and in-depth inquiries of God will facilitate progress in the acquisition of knowledge. God being the knower of past, present and future, and the redeemer, dictates when each being will receive this knowledge.

4-40
ajnas c'sraddadhānas ca
samsayātmā vinasyati
nā 'yam loko'sti na paro
na sukham samsayātmanah

The ignorant, the man devoid of sraddha, the doubting self, goes to destruction. They neither attain this world, the next or happiness.

Unless one has the faith like that of a baby he cannot gain access to God. By not trusting the words and deeds of the good people he alienates himself and so falls by the wayside.

6-37
ayatih sraddhayo 'peto
yogāc calitamānasah
aprāpya yogasamsiddhim
kām gatim krsna gacchati

Arjuna said

Oh Krishna - What happens to the faithful who due to lack of diligence fails to fully qualify?

16-1
sri bhagavān uvāca
abhayam sattvasamsuddhir
jnānayogavyavasthitih
dānam damash ca yajnash ca
svādhyāyas tapa ārjavam

Fearlessness, purity of mind, wise apportionment of knowledge and concentration, charity, self-control and sacrifice, study of the scriptures, austerity and uprightness are divine qualities.

Sacrifice - *is the science of giving that which will be beneficial to the masses and at the same time, removing all traces of selfishness from the giver.*

Almsgiving - *to deserving people with genuine love, kindness and humility increases the coffers of the giver by manifolds.*

Austerity - *is the act of recasting one's mind, against his mode of life so as to make him spiritual.*

18-71   ***shraddhāvān anasuyash ca***
                               shrinuyād api yo narah
                               so'pi muktah shubhāmllokān
                               prāpnuyāt punyakarmanām

If a man simply listens to it with faith and without malice, he, too, will be freed from his sins and repair to the heaven of the righteous.

Being an expert at academic explanation and not following it has no spiritual value. However the person who listens to it and follows even a little, will reap the appropriate fruit. The essence of religion lies in its practice and realization.

"Spirituality is not something to be gained by scriptural studies or hearsay. Mad indeed is the one who thinks of unraveling the mysteries of spiritual life with the help of a mind torn by passions, tyrannized by the senses and agonized by carnal hankerings" Swami Pranavananda.

FAITH - SACRIFICE, AUSTERITY AND CHARITY

The following slokas pertain to more than one of the faiths that are mentioned in this section. As such they are grouped together so as to avoid repetition. When the individual sections are read please include these slokas.

8-28

> *vedeshu yajneshu tapahsu cai 'va*
> *dāneshu yat punyaphalam pradishtam*
> *atyeti tat sarvam idam viditvā*
> *yogi param sthānam upaiti cā 'dyam*

Knowing the merits accrued from recitation of the scriptures, performance of austerities and charities and by knowing and observing the answers to the seven questions raised in this chapter the yogin rises above everything to the realm of the primal cause-the feet of Brahma.

9-27

> *yat karoshi yad ashnāsi*
> *yaj juhosi dadāsi yat*
> *yat tapssyasi kaunteya*
> *tat kurusva madarpanam*

O Son of Kunti (Arjuna), whatever thou doest, eatest or giveth, whatever thou offerest as sacrifice and whatever austerities thou performest, do that as an offering unto Me.

Sri Ramakrishna usually prayed to Mother Kali "My doings are all your doings, not I, not I but you". At Bharat Sevashram Sangha surrender, detachment and celibacy are necessary for spiritual progress. These are all aids to better dedication of one's life to serve society. However, serving society and these austerities are just means to self-realization and not the goal.

10-5

> *ahimsā samatā tushtis*
> *tapo dānam yasho 'yashah*
> *bhavanti bhāvā bhutānām*
> *matta eva prithagvidhāh*

Non-violence, equal-mindedness, contentment, austerity, charity fame and infamy the different states of beings all proceed from Me alone.

Equanimity - *the lack of likes or dislikes during or after desirable or undesirable happenings.*

Austerity - *elimination of bad habits through rigorous self-discipline.*

Charity - *the giving of good and useful things to the deserving*

By the grace of God, all these powers have been bestowed to the disciple.

11-48   *na vedayajnādhyayanair na dānair*
                na ca kriyābhir na tapobhir ugraih
                evam rupah shakya aham nriloke
                drashtum tvadanyena kurupravira

O great hero of the Kurus (Arjuna), I cannot be seen in this form in this mortal world through the study of the Vedas, or practice of rituals, sacrifices or severe austerities, or by any one else other than thee.

Arjuna by surrendering to the Lord, received in return an abundance of His grace. All rituals and academic learning are good for spiritual life but are tainted with egoism.

17-5   *ashāstravihitam ghoram*
                tapyante ye tapo janāh
                dambhāhamkārasamyuktāh
                kāmarāgabalānvitah

17-6   *karshayantah sharirastham*
                bhutagrāmam acetasah
                mām cai 'vā 'ntahsharirastham
                tān viddhy āsuranishcayān

Those who do not have conscience are ruled by arrogance, pride and greed. They cause suffering to the senses in the body and to Me who is the witness and ruler in the intellect. They go against Me, against the scriptures and the good works performed by others. They are demonic forces of disharmony. **(5 & 6)**

The title Jivatma connotes that the aspirant is bounded and controlled by the gunas and through this ignorance the five senses and the mind are born. His existence, he feels is to properly react to the environment and to the external world. This feeling causes bondage to the sensual pleasures, therefore repeated births. The Jivatma is never given a chance to be the controlling factor; it only remains as the witness. The covering shell that the gunas have formed over the Atma has to be cracked and broken to pieces and then the individual self will be revealed.(exp. 5 & 6)

17-24   ***tasmād om ityudāhritya***
            yajna-dāna tapah kriyāh
            pravartante vidhānoktah
            satatam brahmavādinām

Therefore the acts of sacrifice, gift and austerity laid down in the scriptures are always undertaken, uttering the word "Om", by the devotees of Brahman.

Lord Ganesh, the embodiment of the Om, is worshipped as Vighnesvara, the deity that removes obstacles and evils from one's path. As all karma or charity is imperfect when the word Om is repeated, the karma becomes pure and brought in line with nature's plan. All sound originates from Om, all sounds merge in Om. The utterance of Om aids the soul in its evolution to perfection or in the union with the cosmic soul.

17-25   ***tad ityanabhisandhāya***
            phalam yajnatapah kriyāh
            dānakriyāsh ca vividhāh
            kriyante mokshakānkshibhih

The seekers of deliverance perform acts of sacrifice, austerity and charity uttering first the word 'Tat' without the idea of getting any return.*When the word 'tat' is uttered at the time of engaging in sacrifice, austerity and gift giving that act belongs to Isvara. The giver consciously submits himself/herself as an instrument in the hands of the Lord. This leads to salvation*

17-26   ***sadbhāve sādhubhāve ca***
            sad ity etat prayujyate
            prasaste karmani tathā
            sacchabdah pārtha yujyate

The word "Sat" is used in the sense of reality and of goodness; and so also, O Partha, the word "Sat" is used in the sense of an auspicious act.

17-27   *yajne tapasi dāne ca*
                         sthitih sad iti co 'cyate
                         karma cai 'va tadarthiyam
                         sad ity evā 'bhidhiyate

Steadfastness in sacrifice, austerity and gift is also called "Sat" and action for the sake of the Lord is also called "Sat".

If the intent is good, but by ignorance the method is incorrect then by uttering 'Sat', it gets purified. When Sat is uttered, it creates and draws one's mind to think of the reality of God in his state before creation. Sacrifice, austerity and gifts are done to purify the individual, thereby taking him a step closer to Godhood. Any mistake(s) made in this means that the end "can be set right" by uttering 'Sat'.

17-28   **asraddhayā hutam dattam**
                         tapas taptam krtam ca yat
                         asad ity ucyate pārtha
                         na ca tat pretya no iha

Whatever is sacrificed, given or performed and whatever austerity is practiced without faith, is called Asat, O Partha. It is of no account here or hereafter.

Wealth placed in the hands of one lacking in faith is squandered it in no time. Education and earning of money without faith produces a feeling of un-fulfilment of life. Sacrifice, austerity and gift giving are the means of expression of the faith of man and his nature. All his wrong actions are negated. If the individual, who is ignorant of the scriptures utters "Om tat sat".

18-5   **yajnadānatapahkarma**
                         na tyājyam kāryam eva tat
                         yajno dānam tapas cai 'va
                         pāvanāni manishinām

Acts of sacrifice, gifts and austerity should not be abandoned, but performed. Sacrifice, gift and austerity purify the wise.

After his self-education by fulfilling his kamya karma (worldly desires), the aspirant comes to realize the limitations of the world. It is now time to break the cocoon of earthly life and fly freely in the bliss of divine life. His duties are restricted to teaching the world through sacrifice, donating and giving and through austerity or control of the senses.

FAITH - WORSHIP

7-21
> *yo-yo yām-yām tanum bhaktah*
> *sraddhayā 'rcitum icchati*
> *tasyā-tasyā 'calām sraddhām*
> *tām eva vidadhāmy aham*

Whatever celestial form a devotee seeks to worship with reverence, I appear to him in that form.

Worship of God as one perceives Him is not harmful as this keeps the devotee God minded. However, it is only a stepping-stone that will eventually lead to the supreme God.

7-22
> *sa tayā sraddhayā yuktas*
> *tasyā, rādhanam ihate*
> *labhate ca tatah kāmān*
> *mayai 'va vihitān hi tān*

Endowed with that faith, he engages in the worship of that form, and from it he obtains his desires, which are being actually ordained by Me.

Men of mediocre understanding think that the deity worshiped is the giver when in fact the supreme consciousness is the original source. The wisdom of the gurus is really the inspiration of God.

9-23
> *ye 'py anyadevatābhaktā*
> *yajante sraddhay ānvitāh*
> *te 'pi mām eva kaunteya*
> *yajanty avidhipurvakam*

O Son of Kunti (Arjuna), the devotees who worship other Gods with due reverence actually worship Me in fact, though not in the right way.

The powers that minor Gods have infact come from Isvara. The boons bestowed by minor Gods bind man to the cycle of birth and death.

Just like an officer of a Govt. can administer for the welfare of the citizens, in the same manner lesser Gods fulfil the needs of the devotees. They are not doing a favor but merely following the laws of the supreme God; the disciple rightly deserves the grace. No deity can bestow boons without the Lord's grace.

12-2
sri bhagavān uvāca
mayy āveshya mano ye mām
nityayuktā upāsate
shraddhayā parayo 'petās
te me yuktatamā matāh

The Lord said:Those who have fixed their minds on Me, and who are ever steadfast and endowed with supreme Sraddha, worship Me. Them do I consider perfect in yoga.

All paths lead to the same. Worship of God with form or without form will bring self-realization. However, absolute faith and one pointed-ness towards the Lord will lead to the perfect Yoga.

12-20
ye tu dharmāmritam idām
yathoktam paryupāsate
sraddhadhānā matparamā
bhaktās te 'tiva me priyāh

They, who verily, follow this immortal dharma with Sraddha, and devotedly look upon Me as the Supreme Goal, are exceedingly dear to Me.

Prem bhakti is when the devotee gives himself over to the Lord completely. He has gone to places of pilgrimages and done all ritualistic worship, thereby gained faith, contentment and fulfilment. He has gained inward spiritual strength and does not look for anything outside.

17-4
yajante sāttvikā devān
yaksharakshāmsi rājasāh
pretān bhutaganams cā'nye
yajante tāmasā janāh

Men of sattvic temperament worship gods, those of rajasic temperament worship demigods and demons and the tamasic worship hordes of spirits and ghosts

"Show me your company and I will tell you who you are". Good people worship the Lord in the form of Shiva, Ganesh, etc. The passionate worships the deities that is of his own temperament e.g. full of revenge or anger while, the lazy worship the spirits that tease and hurt people.

17-23
om tat sad iti nirdesho
brahmanas trividhah smritah
brāhmanās tena vedās ca
yajnās ca vihitāh purā

"Om Tat Sat" - is taken to be the threefold designation of Brahman. By this in days of yore the Veda-knowing Brahmins, the Vedas and the sacrifices were created.

Om or nada Brahman is the total of all sound. "Tat" means "it", SAT means reality not affected by time, space and causation. The learned, the scriptures and sacrifice are the outcome of Om Tat Sat or the all-conscious original God. Therefore, engaging oneself with sincerity and devotion leads to moksha or liberation.

Also read slokas - 17-24, 25, 26, 27 & 28 from faith

FAITH - SACRIFICE

The greatness of sacrifice

3-9   *y ajnārthāt karmano 'nyatra*
loko 'yam karmabandhanah
tadartham karma kaunteya
muktasangah samācara

Unless work is performed as sacrifice, people lapse into the bondage of work. Hence, O Son of Kunti, perform thy work as a sacrifice, shaking yourself free from all attachments.

Life's fulfillment can be classified in three ways –

- Competition	*- physical level*
- Cooperation	*- mental plane*
- Self-dedication	*- spiritual and ethical plane*

Survival of the fittest is the essence of competition and it is present in all, from animals to plants.

In cooperation, cruel competition becomes less. Instead intelligence, social and gregarious instincts govern the growth and progress. Collective peace and serenity is cultivated for the advancement to upper life.

Self-dedication for the welfare of creation is possessed only by a few enlightened souls. They lift mankind through their example of sharing their knowledge. These enlightened ones are the true performers of selfless service. In the cooperative plane, sharing one's earning by paying due wages and providing enough for law and order for the eradication of the wicked people is Yajna or sacrifice. This attitude of the enlightened and generous people shows the path.

3-11   *devān bhāvayatā 'nena*
te devā bhāvayantu vah
parasparam bhāvayantah
shreya param avāpsyatha

By this sacrifice, thou wilt foster the Gods and they in their turn, will foster thee. Thus by fostering one another, thou will attain the highest good.

The good and noble ones are here to serve good-doers and promote their noble causes. The devotee who trains his senses (Deva) to serve these souls, in turn acquires God-like qualities. Fuel becomes fire when thrown into fire and likewise the devotee becomes one with God with complete surrender.

3-12 **ishtān bhogān hi vo devā
dāsyante yajnabhāvitāh
tair dattān apradāyai 'bhyo
yo bhunkte stena eva sah**

The Gods, nourished by these sacrifices, will offer thee the pleasures thou seek. One who enjoys their gifts without making a return is verily a thief.

The world provides facilities because of sacrifice of few people. The mother makes many sacrifices for the sake of her child's bodily requirements of food, clothing and education. Since we take the sacrifices of others we have to contribute, otherwise we become thieves.

3-13 **yajnashishtāsinah santo
mucyante sarvakilbishaih
bhunjate te tv agham pāpā
ye pacanty ātmakāranāt**

The good people who feed upon the left-overs of the sacrifice, are absolved of all sins. But the unrighteous who cook only for themselves feed on sins.

Work is neither good nor bad but the motive makes it good or bad. If there is no selfish or egotist motive it is purely for the welfare of the masses. It is good. King Yudhisthira of the Mahabharata once invited hundreds of people from all walks of society with intent of feeding and giving them gifts but his motive was not intense and sincere enough as demonstrated by the mongoose. It was done, for pomp and glory.

There are five types (Pancha yajna) of sacrifices; they form obligatory duties of man.

Deva Yajna	- *worship of Gods*
Rishi Yajna	- *worship of enlightened souls - books*
Pitri Yajna	*worship of living parents and departed ancestors*
Nara Yajna	- *devoted service to mankind*
Bhuta Yajna	- *relationship and caring for all living beings*

As God has entered in all His creation as the soul, the five elements are the lower self. Performance of these Yajnas or sacrifices is a constant reminder that God is always present.

The wheel of life (14,15,16)

3-14   *annād bhavanti bhutāni*
                          parjanyād annasambhavah
                          yajnād bhavati parjanyo
                          yajnah karmasamudbhavah

From food come the creatures, from rain comes the food, from sacrifice comes rain and sacrifice comes from action.

The performance of the fire sacrifice has two benefits. The burning of the specially selected herbs and roots etc. act as a cleansing agent for the air and at the same time carbon dioxide is produced, beneficial for plants. Secondly, a subtle mental force is emanated which induces rainfall.

3-15   *karma brahmodbhavam viddhi*
                          brahmā 'ksharasamudbhavam
                          tasmāt sarvagatam brahma
                          nityam yajne pratisthitam

Know this that action derives from the Vedas (Brahma), the Vedas derive from the Imperishable One. Hence the all-pervading Brahma is ever enshrined at the place of sacrifice.

When Karma or duty is performed perfectly and with the right motive, it becomes sacrifice. When the inhabitants of the universe take to sacrifice then the universe becomes elated and becomes a heavenly place.

3-16   *evam pravartitam cakram*
                          nā 'nuvartayati 'ha yah
                          aghāyur indriyārāmo
                          mogham pārtha sa jivati

He who does not follow the wheel thus set turning round and round is a sensualist and lives a vile life. O Partha, he lives his life to no purpose.

The wheel of nature is setup by the Lord for nursing, training, disciplining and elevating all beings at varying levels of existence. If a person does not perform his or her inherent duties, then he becomes a burden or dead weight to society. He causes disharmony in his own little way to the progress of self-realization and universal emancipation.

Different types of sacrifices (23-33)

4-23
gatasamgasya muktasya
jnānāvasthitacetasah
yajnāyā 'caratah karma
samagram praviliyate

He whose attachment has disappeared, whose mind rests secure in knowledge and who works in the spirit of sacrifice - all his actions dissolve away.

Seek the protection of God first by equipping yourself with self-knowledge before you acquire wealth for it will be the cause of your bondage.

4-25
daivam evā 'pare yajnam
yoginah paryupāsate
brahmāgnāv apare yajnam
yajnenai 'vo 'pajuhvati

Some yogins offer sacrifices to the Gods, while others offer sacrifices into the flame of Brahma by means of the sacrifice itself (or by offering self by the self alone).

4-30
apare niyatāhārāh
prānān prānesu juhvati
sarve 'py ete yajnavido
yajnaksapitakalmashāh

Still others of regulated food habit offer in the pranas the functions thereof. All these are knowers of Yajna, having their sins destroyed by

Yajna.*All living beings get their nourishment from plants or animals. Yajna removes the sin that is accrued by this process.*

4-31

yajnashishtāmritabhujo
yānti brahma sanātanam
nā 'yam loko 'sty ayajnāsya
kuto 'nyah kurusattama

The eaters of the nectar, the remnants of Yajna go to the Eternal Brahman. If this world is not for the non-sacrificer, how then the other, O best of the Kurus?

The greatest sacrifice is to crucify the Jivahoodness. Then the divine or Brahma hood will take its place.

4-32

evam bahuvidhā yajnā
vitatā brahmano mukhe
karmajān viddhi tān sarvān
evam jnātvā vimokshyase

Many such forms of sacrifice have been set forth in detail through the lips of Brahman. Know this that all these derive from action. Knowing thus, thou shalt be set free.

Veda is the study of the functions of Nature and Nature is the embodiment of Karma. To convert karma into sacrifice is to conform to the sacred plan of Nature which is to seek liberation

4-33

sreyān dravyamayād yajnāj
jnānayajnāh paramtapa
sarvam karmā 'khilam pārtha
jnāne parisamāpyate

O Scourge of Foes, yajna in the form of knowledge is superior to yajna performed with material things. Know thou this, O Partha, that all actions in their totality, find their culmination and completeness, in knowledge of the Divine.

Accumulation of wealth, of more than what is actually required, causes anxiety and draws the individual away from the acquisition of intelligence. "It is easier for a camel to pass through the eye of a needle than a rich man to enter into heaven." A balance of wealth and knowledge leads to wisdom of what is real and what is unreal.

5-29
bhoktāram yajnatapasām
sarvalokamaheshvaram
suhridam sarvabhutānām
jnātvā mām shāntim ricchati

Having known me as the partaker of sacrifices and spiritual strivings, the Sovereign Lord of the worlds and the Friend of all creatures, he (the sage) attains peace.

It is only though the grace of the Lord and performance of Yoga we can go to liberation. God in turn grants wisdom and the appropriate fruits of our actions. Just thinking of His greatness gives one peace.

9-16
aham kratur aham yajnah
svadhā 'ham aham aushadham
mantroham aham evājyam
aham agnir aham hutam

I am the Vedic ritual, I am the sacrifice, I am the oblation to manes, I am the medicinal herb, I am the hymn, I am the sacrificial butter, I am the sacred fire and the offering.

God is everything, nothing exists without Him; yajna is the Vedic sacrifice of giving our self to the universal Self. The gift and the surrender are both His.

9-20
traividyā mām somapāh putapāpā
yajnair istvā svargatim prārthayante
te punyam āsādya surendralokam
ashnanti divyān divi devabhogān

The adepts in the three Vedas who worship Me by performing sacrifices are cleansed of sin by drinking the soma juice. They pray to be received in heaven. They attain the holy domain of the king of heaven and savor of the pleasures of the Gods.

The Vedas lead one to the path as described by this sloka and not union with the cosmic Consciousness.

10-25   *maharshinām bhrigur aham*
                         girām asmy ekam aksaram
                         yajnānām japayajno 'smi
                         sthāvarānām himālayah

Among the great sages, I am Bhrigu; of words I am the monosyllabic Om;
of sacrifices, I am the sacrifice consisting of japa (silent repetition of the
sacred names of God); and of the immovable, I am the Himalayas.

*Bhrigu is considered to be the highest Rishi born of the mind of God. Utterance
of the monosyllable Om is a sure way to divinity as it is equal to God. Japa is
the easiest of all Yajnas as it can be uttered at any time or at any place. The
vegetable kingdom is classified amongst the moving beings. The Himalayan
Mountains supporting this life is the glory of the Lord.*

17-1   *arjuna uvacā*
                         ye sastravidhim utsrjya
                         yajante sraddhayā 'nvitāh
                         tesām nisthā tu kā krsna
                         sattvam āho rajas tamah

Arjuna said:What is the nature of the devotion of those, O Krishna, who
though disregarding the ordinance of the Sastras, perform sacrifice with
Sraddha? Is it one of Sattva, Rajas or Tamas?

*Many people possess very little knowledge of the scriptures but with inherent
faith, void of lust, greed and anger, are worshipping deities with pure motives.
Arjuna is inquiring about them.*

17-2   *sri bhagavān uvāca*
                         trividhā bhavati sraddhā
                         dehinām sā svabhāvaja
                         sāttviki rājasi cai 'va
                         tāmasi ce 'ti tām srnu

The Lord said:The faith of the embodied is of these kinds, born of their
nature - the Sattvika, the Rajasic and the Tamasika. Hear now about it.
*Tendencies of previous births reappear in ones personality, as they are evident
in his/her words and deeds. These are goodness, passionate-ness and laziness.*

17-3

sattvānurupa sarvasya
sraddhā bhavati bhārata
sraddhāmayo 'yam puruso
yo yacchraddhah sa eva sah

The sraddha of every man, O Bharata, is in accordance with his natural disposition. Man is of the nature of his sraddha; what his sraddha is, that verily he is.

Man, the highest of all beings, has his free will at his disposal. Lower beings have less of a free will. When the free will leads one to salvation, it is called faith (sraddha). One endowed with faith, develops confidence in himself and goes about his duties, and quest for realization with zeal by translating the ideal into practice.

As in the case of Nachiketa, the all inclusiveness of his faith was fully expressed by the boon he asked of Yama, the Lord of death.

First wish - *redemption of his father.*

Second wish - *sought ways and means of earning earthly prosperity and enjoyment.*

Third wish - *sought supreme knowledge from the God of death.*

17-7

āhāras tv api sarvasya
trividho bhavati priyah
yajnas tapas tathā dānam
teshām bhedam imam shrinu

The food which is agreeable to different men is also of three kinds. So, too, are the kinds of sacrifices, austerities and charities. Listen now to their distinctions.

17-11

aphalākānkshibhir yajno
vidhidishto ya ijyate
yashtavyam eve 'ti manah
samādhāya sa sāttvikah

The sattvic sacrifice is the one which is offered, conforming to the scriptural rules, by those who look for no reward, firmly convinced that it is incumbent on them to offer the sacrifice.

When a Yajna is done as adoration to the Lord, in accordance with the
scriptures and no reward is expected then that yajna is sattvika or goodness.

17-12   **abhisandhāya tu phalam**
                       dambhāratham api cai 'va yat
                       ijyate bharatashreshtha
                       tam yajnam viddhi rājasam

But, O Best of Bharatas (Arjuna), that which is offered with an eye on
reward or for pompous display, know that to be rajasic.

When the yajna is done for glorification, showmanship and done in the spirit
of bartering that yajna is harmful and therefore rajasika.

17-13   **vidhihinam asrishtānnam**
                       mantrahinam adakkshinam
                       sraddhāvirahitam yajnam
                       tāmasam paricakshate

The sacrifice which is performed without regard to scriptural injunctions,
in which no food is distributed, no hymns chanted, no sacrificial fee paid
and which is devoid of faith, is called tamasic.

Mantras (spiritually charged words) are the external indications of the solemn
determination and noble intent behind any action. Mechanical recitation of
mantras during sacrifices has little value. Gifts must be given to those who
participate with the sincere intensity by the giver. Faith in God must be the
thought at the time otherwise the act is tamasika.

Please read slokas - Faith - sacrifice,austerity and charity - Page 61.

FAITH - FOOD

4-24
brahmā 'rpanam brahma havir
brahmāgnau brahmanā hutam
brahmai 'va tena gantavyam
brahmakarma samādhinā

The oblation is Brahman, the clarified butter is Brahman, offered by Brahman in the fire of Brahman; unto Brahman verily he goes who cognizes Brahman alone in his action.

The ordinary man upon offering this prayer, sees the items used as matters. However, the enlightened one realizes the oneness or Brahman in all of them.

6-16
nā 'tyasnatas tu yogo 'sti
na cai 'kāntam anasnatah
na cā 'tisvapnasilasya
jāgrato nai 'va cā 'rjuna

Yoga is not possible for him who eats too much or for him who abstains too from eating; it is not for him, O Arjuna, who sleeps too much or too little.

Overeating causes laziness while under eating causes weakness, moderate eating of right food promotes fulfilment of spiritual life.

17-7
āhāras tv api sarvasya
trividho bhavati priyah
yajnas tapas tathā dānam
teshām bhedam imam shrinu

The food, which is agreeable to different men, is also of three kinds. So, too, are the kinds of sacrifices, austerities and gifts. Listen now to their distinctions.

17-8
āyuhsattvabalārogya
sukha-priti-vivardhanāh
rasyāh snigdhāh sthirā hridyā
āhārāh sāttvikapriyāh

The foods, which enhance life force, energy, strength, health, joy and cheerfulness, are sweet, bland, nourishing and pleasant and are dear to those of sattvic nature.

Eat as much as you require during midday meal.

Reduce night meal as much as possible.

Breakfast should be fairly light but eaten regularly.

Eat food that will aid in maintaining body temperature that is warm food in cold seasons and cold food in warm seasons.

Eat food that does not cause discomfort to the digestive system, are easily digestible and nutritive.

17-9   **katvamla lavanātyushna**
                              tikshna-ruksha-vidāhinah
                              āhārā rājasasye 'shtā
                              duhkha-shokāmayapradāh

The food that is bitter, sour, salty, over-hot, pungent, dry and burning, that which cause pain, grief and disease, are dear to men of rajasic nature.

Food that tortures by causing bloodshot watery eyes, running nose, burning stomach and tingling of the tongue, causes distraction from meditation.

17-10   **yātayāmam gatarasam**
                              puti paryushitam ca yat
                              ucchishtam api cā 'medhyam
                              bhojanam tāmasapriyam

Food cooked overnight, insipid, putrid, stale, leftover and impure, is dear to men of tamasic nature.

The food that we like and eat is directly related to our behavior and nature. Food that is eaten from another's plate or tasted by others is tamasika.

Also read slokas - 17-24, 25, 26, 27 & 28 from faith.

FAITH - AUSTERITY

4-28
dravyayajnās tapoyajnā
yogayajnās tathā 'pare
svādhyāya-jnānayajnas ca
yatayah samsitavratāh

Some offer as sacrifice their worldly goods or their austerities or their yogic practices, such as breath-control or some chaste rigorous souls offer their study and scholarship of the holy text of the Vedas.

Man reforms himself through austerity and self-purification. Sincere and devotional offerings are replenished in manifold by the Lord, for example, he who preaches the Geeta receives the essence of it both academically and spiritually.

7-9
punyo gandhah prithivyām ca
tejas cā 'smi vibhāvasau
jivanam sarvabhuteshu
taps cā 'smi tapasvishu

I am the sacred fragrance of the earth and radiance of the fire. I am the life in all beings and austerity in ascetics.

Fire and sun is a reminder of the ever splendor of the Lord. Meditation on them sparks the everlasting bliss of the soul in man, and eventually freedom from death. Austerity is the act of intensifying one's life to achieve self-realization. The Lord sanctions and grants His grace on these acts. Lord is famous for His severe austerity and so given the name Ghora Tapasvin

17-14
devadvija guru prājna
pujanam saucam ārjavam
brahmacaryam ahimsā ca
shāriram tapa ucyate

Reverence for the Gods, Brahmins, preceptors and the wise, purity, uprightness, continence and non-violence - these are the virtues, the practice of which is called the austerity of the body.

The teachers are they who set an example of spiritual life through their personal careers. They have re-cast the moulds of their lives through austerity. They have elevated themselves by getting rid of base habits of the body, mind and speech.

The aspirant worshipping these great souls, gets himself re-cast in the divine mould. Uprightness is to execute all bodily activities in a clean, open and ethical way. Continence is when the thoughts, words and deeds are removed from the senses and sensual pleasure and are made to only serve God.

17-15
> **anudvegakaram vākyam**
> **satyam priyahitam ca yat**
> **svādhyāyābhyasanam cai 'va**
> **vānmayam tapa ucyate**

By austerity of speech is meant use of words that do not generate excitement, that are true, full of love, goodness and are from the Vedic scriptures.

Words that hurt should be avoided however, lies should not be told. Instead, truth should be told in a mild manner. Flattery and false complements should be avoided. Only words that benefit should be uttered.

Daily rhythmic chanting from the Geeta, Upanishads, chandipath etc., creates and maintains spiritual discipline.

17-16
> **manah prasādah saumyatvam**
> **maunam ātmavinigrahah**
> **bhāvasamsuddhir ity etat**
> **tapo mānasam ucyate**

The practice of serenity, gentleness, reticence, self-discipline and purity of mind is called the austerity of mind.

Serenity *of mind is the lack of depression, and confusion while the mind is made to be occupied on blissful thoughts.*

Kindness *is gentleness.*

Silence *is the freedom from meditating on pairs of opposites.*

Self-control *is permitting only the pure noble thoughts to occupy the mind. From a noble mind comes noble words and deeds.*

17-17
> **shraddhayā parayā taptam**
> **tapas tat trividham naraih**
> **aphalākānkshibhir yuktaih**
> **sāttvikam paricakshate**

Physical, verbal and mental austerities practised by serene poised aspirants who are indifferent to the fruits of their action is known as sattvic austerity.

Austerity of mind, body and speech is a continuous process and if no reward is expected it is sattvika.

17-18
    satkāra māna pujārtham
    tapo dambhena cai 'va yat
    kriyate tad iha proktam
    rājasam calam adhruvam

That austerity which is ostentatiously performed with the object of winning respect, honour is called rajasic. It is fleeting and its effect is not lasting.

The three fold austerities practiced only for a short period of time just for public show is rajasika. This has no spiritual value, if it is done only for worldly glamour and hypocritical status.

17-19
    mudhagrāhenā 'tmano yat
    pidayā kriyate tapah
    parasyo 'tsādanārtham vā
    tat tāmasam udāhritam

Austerity is said to be tamasic in nature when it is practised through a deluded understanding, by means of self-torture or for causing injury to others.

The intellects of people of tamasika nature are not fully developed and so their ability to understand ideals is imperfect. Their understanding of austerity is to torture the senses by exposing the body to extreme heat, cold and starvation, not knowing what the result will be. Occasionally they may get some psychic power, which they use to torment fellow humans.

18-42
    shamo damastapah shaucam
    kshāntir ārjavameva ca
    jnānam vijnānamāstikyam
    brahmakarma svabhāvajam

A Brahmana's duties, born of his nature, are control of mind and senses, austerity, purity, forgiveness, simplicity, wisdom, realization and faith in God.

Serenity - *peacefulness of mind emanating from realization*

Self-restraint - *lack of irrational response due to sense control and self control;*

Austerity - *to control of body, mind and speech*

Purity - *to be established in the original state.*

Forgiveness - *to be accommodating and to refrain from retaliation and mockery of others*

Uprightness - *to seek the welfare of all through thoughts, words and deeds.*

Knowledge - *belief in God and His creation and insight into the God realization.*

Realization - *Knowing the difference between mundane and spiritual; knowing that God is the only reality.*

All the thoughts, words and deeds are motivated by the realization that the life continues after death. The Brahmans possessions are just enough for his basic needs and his sojourn on earth is the like that of a pilgrim. His presence together with other Brahmans lifts society to spiritual heights

Please read slokas - Faith - sacrifice, austerity and charity - Page 61.

FAITH - CHARITY

3-12
ishtān bhogān hi vo devā
dāsyante yajnabhāvitāh
tair dattān apradāyai 'bhyo
yo bhunkte stena eva sah

The Gods, nourished by these sacrifices, will offer thee the pleasures thou seek. One who enjoys their gifts without making a return is verily a thief.

The world provides facilities because of the sacrifice of few people. The mother sacrifices for her baby. Educational institutions, clothing, food etc. are the outcome of sacrifices. Since we take the sacrifices of others we have to contribute, otherwise we become thieves.

16-15
ādhyo 'bhijanavānasmi
ko'nyo'sti sadrisho mayā
yakshye dāshyāmi modishye
ityajnānavimohitāh

Bound by hundreds of ties of desire, given over to lust and anger, they strive to amass hoards of wealth, by unjust means, for the gratification of their desires.

17-7
āhāras tv api sarvasya
trividho bhavati priyah
yajnas tapas tathā dānam
teshām bhedam imam shrinu

The food, which is agreeable to different men, is also of three kinds. So, too, are the kinds of sacrifices, austerities and gifts. Listen now to their distinctions.

17-13
vidhihinam asrishtānnam
mantrahinam adakshinam
sraddhāvirahitam yajnam
tāmasam paricakshate

The sacrifice, which is performed without regard to scriptural injunctions, in which no food is distributed, no hymns chanted, no sacrificial fee paid and which is devoid of faith, is called *tamasic.*

Mantras (spiritually charged words) are the external indications of the solemn determination and noble intent behind any action. Mechanical recitation of mantras during sacrifices has little value. Gifts must be given to those who participate with the same sincere intensity as the giver. Faith in God must be the thought at the time otherwise the act is tamasika.

17-20   ***dātavyam iti yad dānam***
                             diyate 'nupakārine
                             deshe kāle ca pātre ca
                             tad dānam sāttvikam smritam

That gift, made without looking for a return, with the idea that it is one's duty to give and which is given in the right place and time and to a deserving recipient, is said be sattvic.

The attitude of the giver is more important than the gift itself. A gift that is given –
    -Not expecting a favor or gift in return,
    -To a person not necessarily in position to return the favor,
    -Without show or publicity,
    -Knowledge that it will be used properly,
    -Knowledge of the location of the person (out of locality is not
     recommended),
    -Giving at a time it will be useful,

All these qualities make the act sattvika.

17-21   *yat tu pratyupakārārtham*
                             phalam uddisya vā punah
                             diyate ca pariklishtam
                             tad dānam rājasam smritam

The gift, however, which is grudgingly made with a view to getting a return or making a gain, is said to be rajasic.

A rajasika gift is given -
- *As a public display*
- *Reluctantly and with mental pain*
- *The giver is looking for a gift*
- *Both the giver and the receiver experience mental pain*

17-22   ***adeshakāle yad dānam***
                          apātrebhyas ca diyate
                          asatkritam avajnātam
                          tat tāmasam udāhritam

The gift, which is made at a wrong place or time or to an undeserving party with lack of respect and in contemptuous manner is said to be tamasic.

A tamasika gift is one that is given –
- *To one habitually living in a dirty place, at a time of sleep, or engaged in defecating etc.*
- *To a person of questionable character and who lacking in self control.*
- *Who does not think of the welfare of the society and who squanders money.*
- *When the receiver is treated with disrespect.*
- *When the giver gives with abuse and scolding.*

18-43   ***shauryam tejo dhritir dākshyam***
                          yuddhe cā 'pyapalāyanam
                          dānam ishvarabhāvash ca
                          kshātram karma svabhāvajam

The duties of a Kshatriya, ordained by his nature, are prowess, vigour, steadfastness, skill, and dauntlessness in battle, generosity and command over others.

The Kshatriya is the embodiment of duty and is an ideal man. His duty is to put man's earthly life on the path to realization. In this process, he is not afraid to sacrifice his body and will never accept a life of slavery. The enemy never intimidates the Kshatriya even if he is overpowered, for his firmness and resourcefulness takes him out of difficult situations. He may retreat out of wisdom only with the realization that a later stage he will get an opportunity to act.

Generosity is the maximum of distribution of one's wealth to the deserving masses for their welfare and prosperity. The Kshatriya ensures this. His mental makeup makes him a leader as he upholds the law of the land. He becomes the beacon light for others. Thus he is on the brink of becoming a Brahman.

Please read slokas - Faith - sacrifice,austerity and charity - Page 61.

Guidance of a spiritual master

4-34   *tad vidhi pranipātena*
                        pariprashnena sevayā
                        updeksyanti te jnānam
                        jnāninas tattvadarshinah

Learn that by reverence (prostrating yourself), by questioning, by service. Those seers and the wise ones will teach you that knowledge.

"When the disciple is ready, the Guru will appear". Sat Guru or God in the form of man knows the state of being of every aspirant. He leads the earnest disciples gradually to where they can receive spiritual guidance. The earthly Guru is he who has had experiences of God. Just as a lamp can light another lamp, the Guru will transmit knowledge to the disciple who has prostrated himself at his feel. Through devotion and enquiry at the feet of the teacher regarding real and unreal, bondage and freedom, the disciple will gain insight of spirituality. But dictatorship by the Guru is the sign of a Pseudo Guru.

In the end, the scriptures, the experiences of the mind, experiences during meditation and the direct experiences and dreams must agree. Faith comes first then knowledge, then experience of God. When God bestows His grace of insight and wisdom, the disciple begins to understand reality. The disciple then passes it to the masses, leading to the process of universal emancipation.

17-14   *deva dvija guru prājna*
                        pujanam saucam ārjavam
                        brahmacaryam ahimsā ca
                        shāriram tapa ucyate

Reverence for the Gods, Brahmins, preceptors and the wise, purity, uprightness, continence and non-violence - these are the virtues. The practice of this is called the austerity of the body.

The teachers are they who set an example of spiritual life through their personal careers. They have re-cast the moulds of their lives through austerity. They have elevated themselves by getting rid of base habits of the body, mind and speech. The aspirant worshipping these great souls, get himself re-cast in the divine mould. Uprightness is to execute all bodily activities in a clean, open and ethical way. When the thoughts, words and deeds are removed from sense and sex pleasures and are made to only serve God, then this is called continence.

God's grace

2-8 *na hi prapashyāmi mamā panudyād*
yachchokam ucchoshanam idriyānām
avāpya bhumav asapatnam riddham
rājyam surānām api ca 'dhipatyam

Even if I win for myself a flourishing and unrivalled kingdom on earth and dominion over the Gods I do not see what can relieve the sorrow that is drying up my senses.

The impending war was to regain the kingdom from the Kauravas, Arjuna's first cousins. The thought of killing his blood relations for worldly riches was an excuse for not fighting; all along he was performing duties as a Kshatriaya. The Lord now showed the compassion of a father, a caring mother's love, the king's protection, the firm hand of a spiritual master and most of all His grace.

4-12 **kānkshantah karmanām siddhim**
yajanta iha devatāh
kshipram hi mānushe loke
siddhir bhavati karmajā

Here those who desire success for their action, offer worship to Gods, for success from action comes quickly in this world.

Man can obtain quickly, results that are perceived by his senses but they are temporary. Self-realization, which is the grace of God or Guru, comes to those who ardently seek it.

5-15 *nā 'datte kasyacit pāpam*
na cai 'va sudritam vibhuh
ajnānenā 'vritam jnānam
tena muhyanti jantavah

The all-pervading soul does not share anybody's sin or virtue. Wisdom is shrouded in ignorance; hence it is that created beings fall victims to delusions.

All of creation, including man, is the play of the all-pervading consciousness. Creation is made up of matter, the five elements. Matter cannot affect consciousness or God. God thus is not perturbed by the good and bad of individuals

9-30   ***api cet sudurācāro***
                       bhajate mām ananyabhāk
                       sādhur eva sa mantavyah
                       samyag vyavasito hi sah

Even if a most depraved person worships Me with single-minded devotion, he should be deemed righteous for rightly is he resolved.

In Hinduism, there is no such thing as eternal damnation. It is God's plan to release all embodied souls and reunite them with His all-pervading self (Paramatman). The purpose of the Gita is to show the path. A few will catch the craving for liberation and they will spread it far and wide. God as our very own soul, will controller and spectator. Thereby superseding the mind and intellect requires the grace of God. As in the case of Nityanada and Gouranga, through continuous chanting of the Mahamantra, they attracted many followers who in turn forgot the vulgar things and started to enjoy divine ecstasy.

9-31   ***kshipram bhavati dharmātmā***
                       shashvacchāntim nigacchati
                       kaunteya pratijānihi
                       na me bhaktah pranashyati

This depraved person soon turns into a virtuous one and gains eternal peace. O Son of Kunti (Arjuna), you can safely swear that My devotee never comes to grief.

Faith in the Lord is an indispensable ingredient. It is best to lose all worldly belongings including relationships but faith in God must be maintained. The Pandavas lost their kingdom, their lives were in constant jeopardy, they were taunted and belittled, but in the end they got salvation. (Also Valmiki)

9-32   ***mām hi pārtha vyapāsritya***
                       ye 'pi syuh pāpayonayah
                       striyo vaishyās 'tathā shudrās
                       te 'pi yānti parām gatim

O Partha (Arjuna), women, Vaishyas, Sudras and the base-born are all sure to attain to the supreme goal, if only they take refuge in Me.

In olden times, it was thought that the mind of man was more developed than women (except for a few). It was the same with regards to Vaisyas (business class) and Sudras (working class). But the Lord refutes this by saying - all have the right to liberation. Untouchability is totally dismissed, in the case of Sri Rama using the services of Guha, a boatman from the so called Nishadha low caste, to take Him across the Ganges. (also sabari of Ramayana)

10-9
> **maccittā madgataprāṇā**
> **bodhayantah parasparam**
> **kathayantas ca mām nityam**
> **tushyanti ca ramanti ca**

Their mind is centred in Me, their lives are dedicated to Me. Teaching each other and all the time talking about Me, they are full of happiness and joy.

Mind is attracted to what it likes most. A child craves for the parents because of the good and loving response he gets from them. The devotee by constantly thinking of the Lord and His glories gets absorbed in Him. In the case of lovers, the relationship is selfish. However, the devotee of the Lord invites others to join in the divine ecstasy. Hearing the glories of the Lord over and over does not become stale or boring. Love for the Lord causes freedom while lustful love causes bondage.

10-10
> **teshām satatayuktānām**
> **bhajatām pritipurvakam**
> **dadāmi buddhiyogam tam**
> **yena mām upayanti te**

To them who are in constant union with Me, who worship Me with love, I give the power of knowledge and understanding by which they realize Me.

God reveals himself based on the nature and attainment of the disciple

10-11
> **teshām evā 'nukampārtham**
> **aham ajnānājam tamah**
> **nāshayāmy ātmabhāvastho**
> **jnānadipena bhāsvatā**

Out of compassion for them, I, dwelling in their hearts, dispel the darkness born of ignorance by the radiant lamp of wisdom.

An analogy of the physical lamp can be compared to the lamp of wisdom.

Oil – *is constant discrimination.*

Wick – *is constant practice of continence and meditation which keeps it burning. It can be compared to the awareness of the self (Prajna).*

Shade – *is a protection from gusty winds just as the mind free from attachment and aversion is the best windscreen.*

Flame - *is the unbroken consciousness of the Lord.*

By the grace of the Lord, He will reveal Himself to the deserving devotees that which is unreal.

11-8   **na tu mām shakyase drashtum
                         anenai 'va svacakshusha
                         divyam dadāmi te cakshuh
                         pashya me yogam aishvaram**

But thou canst behold Me with these eyes of yours. I give to thee the divine vision. Behold My marvelous power.

Man with all his progressive mastery over the knowledge of nature has not solved the problems of life and death. Spiritual life fills this void or mystery. Through the grace of God, the spiritual aspirant merges his personal Will with that of the Cosmic Will, thereby becoming a God realized soul. Intuition or the third eye is the fruit of this union. God realization in the various planes of the consciousness –

1. *Mental plain - the phenomenon*
2. *Ethical plain - infallible law*
3. *Divine eye level - kinetic or active God*
4. *Intuitive level - static God*

After these levels, the individuals merge with God. Arjuna was bestowed by God's grace the divine eye and so all his problems disappeared

11-48   *na vedayajnādhyayanair na dānair*
               na ca kriyābhir na tapobhir ugraih
               evam rupah shakya aham nriloke
               drashtum tvadanyena kurupravira

O great hero of the Kurus (Arjuna), I cannot be seen in this form in
this mortal world through the study of the Vedas, or practice of rituals,
sacrifices or severe austerities, or by any one else other than thee.

*Arjuna by surrendering to the Lord, received in return an abundance of His
grace. All rituals and academic learning are good for spiritual life but are
tainted with egoism.*

18-58   *macchittah sarvadurgāni*
                   matprasādāt tarishyasi
                   atha cet tvam ahamkārān
                   na shroshyasi vinankshyasi

With thy mind fixed on Me, thou shalt overcome all difficulties by My
grace. But if for egoism, thou hearest not, thou shalt fall into perdition.

*Man's struggles are of two kinds - internal and external. Technology is constantly
introducing new and easier ways for him to harness nature for his comfort.
However, a beneficial world is of little use to one who has not conquered his
mind. Uncontrolled mind is Satan. Minds that are turned inwards in search
of God, finds Him and then sees Him outwardly in all of creation. Prahlad
accepted his trials and tribulations as doings of the Lord for his speedy self-
realization. With the destruction of egoism, God's grace is given*

18-62   *tam eva saranam gaccha*
                   sarva bhāvena bhārata
                   tatprasādāt parām sāntim
                   sthānam prāpsyasi sāsvatam

Seek refuge in Him alone with all your heart, O Bharata. By His grace you
will gain Supreme Peace and the Eternal Abode.

*Illusions or Maya makes man feel he is the master of his activities when in fact
his only act is to take refuge in the Lord. The physical body is like the waves. It
has no existence of its own. Knowing this as truth the only endeavor is the act
of taking refuge in God. The devotee that takes refuge in the Lord and takes*

natures' lesson as the blessings of God. He performs Karma yoga to stay occupied in thoughts of God and also to stay fit but he knows eternal abode is verily his. The Pandavas took refuge in the lord and they were liberated. Hanumanji and Sabari and so many others took refuge in Sri Rama and they were liberated.

18-66   **sarvadharmān parityajya**
             māmekam sharanam vraja
             aham tvā sarvapāpebhyo
             mokshayishyāmi mā shucah

Abandon all Dharma and take refuge in Me alone. Grieve not, I will deliver thee from all sin and evil.

By surrendering to the Lord the devotee entrusts Him with all the happenings of his/her worldly existence. The Lord in return, protects the disciple when he/she is exposed to dangers and mishaps. Any good or bad that befalls him, he accepts as the doings of the Lord. Seclusion he views as solitude and not loneliness. The devotee's relationship with the Lord is even deeper than the comfort and security that the baby feels in the bosom of the mother.

Taking refuge or self-surrender is this state received by the Karma yogi, the Bhakti yogi and the Jnani. The Yogi merges in the Sat (truth), the Jnani into consciousness (chid), and the Bhakta blooms in ananda (bliss), the pure or original state.

18-73   *arjuna uvāca*
          nasto mohah smritir labdhā
         tvatprasādān maya 'cyuta
         sthito 'smi gatasamdehah
          karisye vacanam tava

Arjuna said:

My delusion is destroyed, I have regained my memory through Your grace, O Achyuta. I am firm; I am free from doubt. I shall act according to your words.

The message of the Gita always stays fresh. Arjuna was transformed as he totally made himself over entirely to the Maker. Like fuel when thrown into fire becomes fire, in like manner Arjuna's personality became one with the Cosmic Personality. When he earlier saw the battle scene, life seemed unbearable.

He could not shake off the deluded feeling neither could he carry it. Now the delusions of birth and death, bondage and freedom and other dualities had vanished. Arjuna lost the memory of his relationship with the original life force that actual exists in him. Intuitive knowledge was regained and realization dawned on him. He surrendered himself as he realized that it was the grace of the Sri Krishna that caused the turn around. He became like a rock, never to fall back to that pitiable state.

Devotion and self-surrender

2-7
kārpanyadoshopahatasvabhāvah
prichchāmi tvām dharmasam mudhacetāh
yachchreyah syān niscitam bruhi tan me
sishyas te 'ham sādhi mām twām prapannam

I am overwhelmed with a sense of pity and guilt. My mind is bewildered, I cannot make out which is the right course of action. I ask thee to tell me for certain which is good for me. I am thy disciple, I am taking refuge in thee. Do enlighten me, I pray.

Arjuna was blessed with the pleasant, preyas, throughout his life. He was learned, he had wealth, wives, offsprings and a kingdom. But in the moment of crisis they were of no use. By surrendering to Sri Krishna he sought Sreyas-goodness.

3-30
mayi sarvāni karmāni
samnyasyā 'dhyātmacetasa
nirāshir nirmano bhutvā
yudhyasva vigatajvarah

Being led by spiritual judgment, resign your actions to Me. Go and fight, giving up desire and egoism and cure yourself of this mental fever.

"Thy will be done" should be the attitude of an aspirant, as God is the owner of everything and the initiator of all activities. Knowing this as truth, adjustment in life must be made.

6-31
sarvabhutasthitam yo mām
bhajaty ekatvam āsthitah
sarvathā vartamāno 'pi
sa yogi mayi vartate

The Yogi who, firmly planted in unity, worships Me as dwelling in all beings, lives in Me whatever be his mode of life.

The senses are mere instruments in the hands of Buddhi or understanding. They get attached to the objects or repulsed. These pairs of opposites govern the behavior of mundane man but for the Godward bound, the senses are pushed aside as they see everything as temporary.

7-1
sri bhagavān uvāca
mayy āsaktamanāh pārtha
yogam yunjan madāsrayah
asamshayam samagram mām
yathā jnāsyasi tac chrinu

The Blessed Lord said:Listen then, O Partha, by practicing yoga with thy mind centered in me and by taking refuge in me, thou shalt come to know me in my entirety without a trace of doubt.

Appreciating the workings of God in His creations is another way of worshipping Him.

7-14
daivi hy esha gunamayi
mama māya duratyayā
mām eva ye prapadyante
māyām etām taranti te

This divine Maya of Mine compounded of the modes of nature is surely difficult to overcome. But those who seek refuge in Me alone can transcend this Maya.

When a rope is seen in the dark, it appears as a snake but on examination the truth is realized. Nature is Daivi Maya (Divine Illusion). Vishnu Bhagawan is nicknamed Mahamaya. Adoration causes the Lord to remove this illusion.

7-15
nā mām duskritino mudhāh
prapadyante narādhamāh
māyayā 'pahritajnānā
āsuram bhāvam āshritāh

The evildoers, being stupid, and being the very dregs of humanity, are besotted by Maya. Demoniac in nature, they do not seek refuge in me.

When the mind and intelligence become the instruments of ego, then evil acts like lying, crookedness, and torture of fellow beings become normal. Moral and ethics are out of the question. They detest the very name of God - let alone worshipping Him.

7-16

caturvidhā bhajante mām
janāh sukritino 'rjuno
ārto jijnāsur arthārthi
jnāni ca bharatarshabha

O Best of Bharatas (Arjuna), the virtuous who worship me belong to four types - distressed ones, knowledge-seekers, wealth-seekers and wise ones.

- *When Draupadi was about to be de-robed in the presence of so many, she called on Sri Krishna and the Lord relieved her distress.*

- *When Swami Vivekananda relentlessly sought knowledge, the Lord gave. Only the few who seek spiritual knowledge receive it.*

- *The Lord provides wealth to the religious-minded easily and without hesitation.*

- *The jnani through the help of the Lord can perceive through intuition, that Brahman is the reality while the universe and the beings are all mere superimpositions on it. Adoring Brahman is His worship.*

These four types of worshippers are virtuous because of their right understanding.

7-17

teshām jnāni nityayukta
ekabhaktir vishishyate
priyo hi jnānino 'tyartham
aham sa ca mama priyah

Among them, the wise one who is ever centred in the Divine, given to single-minded devotion, is the highest, for I am exceedingly dear to him and he to Me.

The Jnani is dearer to the Lord because he sees himself as one with God and creation.

7-28

yesham tv antagatam pāpam
janānām punyakarmanām
te dvandvamohanirmuktā
bhajante mām dridhavratāh

But the doers of good deeds whose sins have been wiped off, being free from delusion born of pairs of opposites, worship me with firm resolve.

Selfless service is a must for continuation and sustenance of a pure mind. What the base mind likes is not necessarily good, so denial will eliminate the pairs of opposites such as gain and loss, victory and defeat, praise and criticism. Only those minds, which are not tainted and are steadfast in their vows, can wholeheartedly worship the Lord, the One in all.

7-29   **jarāmaranamokshāya**
                         mām āshritya yatanti ye
                         te brahma tad viduh kritsnam
                         adhyātmam karma cā 'khilam

Those who strive for freedom from death and infirmities of age, take refuge in Me. Thus will they know Brahman (Absolute), the Self and about action.

Death and decay are staring at him whose mind is unwilling to follow the path of realization. These two factors are constant reminders, and contemplation on them alerts man of the goal of life.

*Swami Pranavanandaji, the Guru of Bharat Sevashram Sangha upon receiving God realization, uttered the ten divine messages of which self-realization is the first(**See Introduction to Gita**). During His short earthly sojourn He spent many nights at the cremation ground deep in meditation so as to teach mankind to think of the ultimate end of this cage of flesh and bones.*

8-14   **ananyacetāh satatam**
                         yo mām smarati nityashah
                         tasyā 'ham sulabhah pārtha
                         nityayuktasya yoginah

O Partha (Arjuna), I am easily attained by a yogin who is always disciplined and who constantly meditates on Me, thinking of nothing else.

Take one step towards the Lord and He takes ten steps towards you.

8-22   **purushah sa parah pārtha**
                         bhaktyā labhyas tv ananyayā
                         yasyā 'ntahsthāni bhutāni
                         yena sarvam idam tatam

O Partha (Arjuna), the Supreme Being in whom all other beings dwell and who pervades this universe, can, however, be attained by single-minded devotion.

Just as the waves are related to the ocean, Jivatma is no separate entity from the ocean of consciousness.

9-13
> *mahātmānas tu mām pārtha*
> *daivim prakritim āshritah*
> *bhajanty ananya-manaso*
> *jnātva bhutādim avyayam*

O Partha (Arjuna), the great souls, possessed of divine nature know Me to be the prime cause of all beings and know me to be imperishable as well. They worship Me with single-minded devotion.

Divine nature (Daivi Prakriti) is opposite to the demonic nature (Mohini Prakriti). The former is born of Sattvika qualities and knows that they have to eventually unite with Paramatman.

9-14
> *satatam kirtayanto mām*
> *yatantas ca dridhavratāh*
> *namasyantas ca mām bhaktyā*
> *nityayuktā upāsate*

Always chanting My glories, firm and persistent in their dedication, devotedly bowing to Me, they worship Me being ever in unison with My spirit.

The holy ones pass their time reading, writing and preaching about the Lord. Their minds are occupied only with thoughts of the Lord. They make vows like being a vegetarian, non-drinker, non-smoker and Brahmacharyam, qualities most helpful for spiritual life.

Man gets what he seeks (9-22 to 9-25)

9-22
> *ananyās cintayanto mām*
> *ye janāh paryupāsate*
> *teshām nityābhiyuktānām*
> *yogakshemam vahāmyaham*

Those who worship Me alone, thinking of none but Me, to these steadfast souls I give all they need and preserve what they have.

When the grace of God is bestowed, God makes sure that the level of existence of the devotee is lifted to spiritual heights. He/she no longer has to toil for food and clothing as God through His grace always maintains this.

9-23   *ye 'py anyadevatābhaktā*
                 yajante sraddhay ānvitāh
                 te 'pi mām eva kaunteya
                 yajanty avidhipurvakam

O Son of Kunti (Arjuna), the devotees who worship other Gods with due reverence also worships Me in fact, though not in the right way.

The power that minor Gods have come from Isvara, but the boons bestowed by minor Gods binds man to the cycle of birth and death.

9-24   *aham hi sarvayajnānām*
                 bhoktā ca prabhur eva ca
                 na tu mām abhijānanti
                 tattvenā 'tascyavanti te

I am alone the partaker and Lord of all sacrifices. But these men know Me not in My true essence and so they fall (fall into rebirth).

In the same way food given by a mother instead of another has a big difference in the build up of the baby. Likewise God's grace by direct worship liberates the aspirant. God is the true enjoyer of sacrifices.

9-25   *yānti devavratā devān*
                 pitrin yānti pitrivratā
                 bhutāni yānti bhutejyā
                 yānti madyājino 'pi mām

Worshippers of the Gods go to the Gods, ancestor-worshippers go to the manes, worshippers of the spirits go to the spirits and My worshippers come unto Me.

Worship of God with form is the easiest (26 & 27)

9-26   *patram pushpam phalam toyam*
                 yo me bhaktyā prajacchati
                 tad aham bhaktyupahritam
                 ashnāmi prayatātmanah

Whatever man gives Me in true devotion whether a leaf, a flower, a fruit
or water, I accept that gift of love from the pure soul.

*Here bhakti devotion is the key as we have seen with the example of Sabari
offering dry fruits to Sri Rama, Sudama offering puffed rice to Sri Krishna
and Vidur offering gruel to the Lord. All in turn received great rewards.*

9-27   *yat karoshi yad ashnāsi*
                     yaj juhosi dadāsi yat
                     yat tapasyasi kaunteya
                     tat kurusva madarpanam

O Son of Kunti (Arjuna), whatever thou doest, eatest or giveth, whatever
thou offerest as sacrifice and whatever austerities thou performest, do that
as an offering unto Me.

*Sri Ramakrishna usually prayed to Mother Kali "My doings are all your doings,
not I, not I but you". At Bharat Sevashram Sangha surrender, detachment and
celibacy are necessities for spiritual progress. These are all aids to better dedicate
one's life to serving society. However, serving society and these austerities are
just means to self-realization and not the goal.*

God loves everyone (9-29 to 9-34)

9-29   *samo 'ham sarvabhuteshu*
                     na me dveshyo 'sti na priyah
                     ye bhajanti tu mām bhaktyā
                     mayi te teshu cā 'py aham

I am alike to all beings. Nobody is hateful or dear to me. But those who
worship Me devotedly dwell in Me and I too dwell in them.

By thinking of and surrendering to God one becomes God like.

9-33   **kim punar bhāhmanāh punyā**
                bhaktā rājarshayas tathā
                anityam asukham lokam
                imam prāpya bhajasva mām

It is needless to speak of the holy Brahmins and devoted royal sages. Do thou worship Me, having been born into this transitory and unhappy world.

From birth to death, every stage of life is a passing through or transitory stage. Today the flowers are beautiful and full of fragrance; tomorrow they are thrown in the rubbish bin because they have withered. In the same way mundane experiences must be cast aside one after the other and ultimately the lasting blessing of union with God will be bestowed.

9-34   **manmanā bhava madbhakto**
                madyāji mām namskuru
                mām evai 'shyasi yuktvai 'vam
                ātmānam matparāyanah

Fill thy mind with Me, be My devotee, worship Me and bow down to Me. Thus steadfastly uniting thy heart with Me alone and making Me thy goal, to Me thou shalt come.

By dedicating oneself to the service of the divine the individual gets utilized maximum by the Lord. He is always attuned to the Cosmic Will or the Will that keeps creation moving steadily towards perfection. Whereas the mundane person seeking personal objects and gratification, is forever attached to trivial experiences. Distress, is inherent in pleasure. In the end, the Yogi forgoes this temporary world and lives in eternal sat-chid-anand.

10-8   **aham sarvasya prabhavo**
                mattah sarvam pravartate
                iti matvā bhajante mām
                budhā bhāvasamanvitāh

I am the origin of all. From Me does everything evolve. Knowing this the wise, filled with love and devotion, worship Me.

Constant thinking of God enriches the mind and makes one a Yogi.

Arjuna praises the lord (11-35 to 11-44)

11-36   *arjuna uvāca*
sthāne hrishikesha tava prakirtyā
jagat prahrishyaty anurajyate ca
rakshāmsi bhitāni disho dravanti
sarve namasyanti ca siddhasamghāh

Arjuna said:O Hrishikesha (Krishna), it is quite in the fitness of things that the world rejoices and is filled with chanting in praise of Thy love. It is therefore also not strange that the Rakshashas flee from Thee in terror in all directions and the hosts of Siddhas (perfected ones) bow down before Thee in adoration.

Each individual sees the Lord based on his degree of evolution. The Rishis are God's closest relations. The spiritually advanced are his friends and the mundane may have some past idea of his existence.

11-37   *kasmāc ca te na nameran mahātam*
gariyase brahmano 'py ādikartre
ananta devesha jagannivasa
tvamaksharam sadasat tat param yat

And why should they not, O Great-soul, bow to You, greater than, the Primal Cause greater than Brahma. O Infinite Being, O Lord of Gods, O Abode of the universe? You are the Imperishable, the Being and the Non-being. You are that which is the Supreme.

Worshipping the Lord in all his aspects the aspirant raises his spiritual state.

11-39   *vāyur jamo 'gnir varunah shashānkah*
prajāpatis tvam prapitāmahashca
namo namas te 'stu sahasrakritvah
punash ca bhuyo 'pi namo namaste

I hail to Thee a thousand times who art Vayu (the wind), Yama (the God of destruction), Agni (Fire), Varuna (the Sea-God) and Shashanka (the moon). My salutations to Thee who art the Lord of Creation (Brahma) and the Supreme grandsire, I bow to Thee again and again.

11-41   *sakhe 'ti matvā prasabham yad uktam*
               he krishna he yādava he sakhe'ti
               ajānatā mahimānam tave'dam
               mayā pramādāt pranayena va'pi

Oh Krishna, O comrade out of negligence and unaware of Thy greatness and may be fondness I have spoken in rashness to Thee, thinking that Thou art my companion.

11-42   *yaccāvahāsārtham asatkritosi*
               vihārashayyāsanabhojaneshu
               eko 'thavā 'py acyuta tatsamaksham
               tat kshāmaye tvām aham aprameyam

In negligent error or love and not knowing this glory and universal form of Thine and looking upon Thee only as a human friend and companion, I have called Thee 'O Krishna, O Yadava, O Comrade'.

On seeing the universal form of the Lord, Arjuna's outlook and address of the Lord changed. He now puts the Lord on the most exalted alter. Swami Atmanandaji of Bharat Sevashram Sangha like all other monks in the beginning, used to see Swami Pranavanandaji as their friend and leader but when in repeated visions, Swamiji saw that the Gods were worshipping Swami Pranavanandaji as their master, his outlook changed. Then he too started to worship his leader and friend as God by performing Aarati. (11-41 & 11-42)
(See Arati Chart)

11-43   *pitāsi lokasya carācarasya*
               tvam asya pujyas ca gurur gariyān
               na tvatsamo 'sty abhyadhikah kuto 'nyo
               lokatraye 'py apratima-prabhāva

Father, Thou art of the universe, moving and unmoving. Thou art the one to be worshipped and the most solemn object of veneration. None is equal to Thee, How can there be one superior to Thee in the three worlds, O Thou, Incomparable in might?

LOGIC OF ARATI

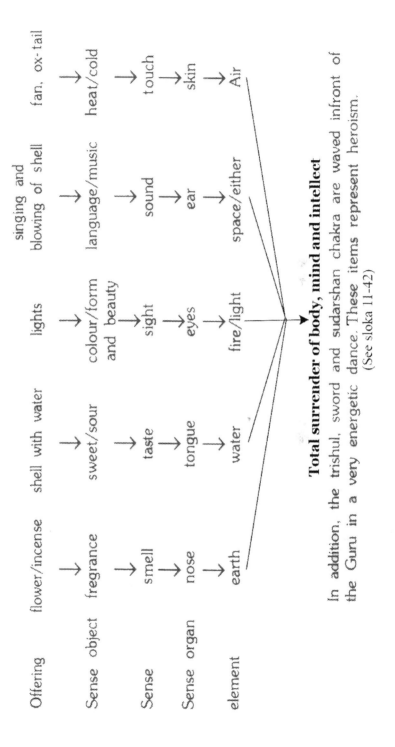

Offering	flower/incense	shell with water	lights	singing and blowing of shell	fan, ox-tail
Sense object	fregrance	sweet/sour	colour/form and beauty	language/music	heat/cold
Sense	smell	taste	sight	sound	touch
Sense organ	nose	tongue	eyes	ear	skin
element	earth	water	fire/light	space/either	Air

Total surrender of body, mind and intellect

In addition, the trishul, sword and sudarshan chakra are waved infront of the Guru in a very energetic dance. These items represent heroism.
(See sloka 11-42)

11-44
> *tasmāt pranamya pranidhāya kāyam*
> *prasādaye tvām aham isham idyam*
> *piteva putrasya sakheva sakhyuh*
> *priyah priyāyārhasi deva sodhum*

Therefore, O Lord, I bow down before Thee and prostrate my self. I pray for Thy grace, Thou Adorable Lord. It behoves Thee to bear with my fault as a father does with his son's, a friend with his friend's, a lover with that of his beloved.

Arjuna pleads to see the gentle form of the Lord (45 and 46)

11-45
> *adrishtapurvam hrishito 'smi drishtvā*
> *bhayena ca pravyathitam mano me*
> *tad eva me darshaya deva rupam*
> *prasica devesha jagannivāsha*

I have seen what was never seen before, and I feel delighted, but my mind is tormented by fear. O Godhead, show me that other form of Thine, O Lord of the Gods, O Refuge of the World. Be gracious.

11-46
> *kiritnam gadinam cakrahastam*
> *icchāmi tvām drashtum aham tathai 'va*
> *tenai 'va rupena caturbhujena*
> *sahasrabāho bhava vishvamurte*

I wish to see Thee as before, with Thy diadem, mace and disc in hand. O Thou of Thousand-arms, O Universal Form, assume that four-armed form of Thine. *Arjuna is used to and happy to see the Lord in His usual two-armed form. He became convinced that this form of His companion was really the god of Gods.*

11-54
> *bhaktyā tv ananyayā shakya*
> *aham evamvidho 'rjuna*
> *jnātum drashtum ca tattvena*
> *praveshtum ca paramtapa*

But by single-minded devotion alone, I can thus be seen in this form and be known in essence and can even be entered into (to be one with the Supreme) O Chastiser of Foes (Arjuna).

Ananya Bhakti is unwavering devotion that is developed first by the divine feeling of the presence of the Lord and then by his darshan or vision (actual vision in wakeful state or true divine vision through meditation and through dreams). Ultimately the Sadhaka merges with the cosmic consciousness.

11-55
**mat karmakrin matparamo
madbhaktah sangavarjitah
nirvairah sarvabhuteshu
yah sa mām eti pāndava**

O Pandava (Arjuna), he who works for Me, regards Me as his goal, worships Me, is totally unattached, bearing enmity to none, comes to Me.

Mind does not cling to two things at the same time. Devotion to the Lord reduces attachment to the world and eventually complete detachment is the result. The love for the Lord must be one-pointed and then all enticements of the world will vanish.

12-1
**arjuna uvāca
evam satatayuktā ye
bhaktās tvām paryupāsate
ye cā 'py aksharam avyaktam
teshām ke yogavittamāh**

Arjuna said: Of the two - those ever-steadfast devotees who worship Thee and those who worship the Imperishable and Unmanifested Brahman - who is the superior devotee?

12-2
**sri bhagavān uvāca
mayy āveshya mano ye mām
nityayuktā upāsate
shraddhayā parayo 'petās
te me yuktatamā matāh**

Those whose minds are attuned to Me in earnest love and who worship Me with supreme faith are deemed by Me to be the highest among the devotees.

All paths lead to the same. Worship of God with form or without form will bring self-realization. However, absolute faith, one pointed-ness towards the Lord will lead to the perfect Yoga.

Worship of God with form (12-6 to 12-10)

12-6   *ye tu sarvāni karmāni*
                       mayi samnyasya matparāh
                       ananyenai 'va yogena
                       mām dhyāyanta upāsate

They lay all their actions on Me, are intent on Me, worship and meditate on Me, with unswerving devotion.

12-7   **teshāmaham samuddhartā**
                       mrityusamsārasāgarāt
                       bhavāmi nacirāt pārtha
                       mayyāveshitacetasām

But those who surrendering all their actions to Me, meditate on Me and worship Me with single-hearted devotion and whose thoughts are centred on Me, O Partha (Arjuna), I rescue these dedicated devotees long from the ocean of mortal existence.

12-8   *mayyeva mana ādhatsva*
                       mayi buddhim niveshaya
                       nivasishyasi mayyeva
                       ata urdhvam na samshayah

So do thou fix thy mind on Me alone, rest thy reason in Me. Hereafter, doubtlessly, thou shalt dwell in Me.

Mind feels while intellect decides. Man is where his mind is. Heaven and hell are states of the mind. Keep the mind on God and then you become God like.

12-9   *atha cittam samādhātum*
                       na shknosi mayi sthiram
                       abhyāsayogena tato
                       mām icchāptum dhanajnaya

O Dhananjaya (Arjuna), if thou failest to fix thy mind steadfastly on Me, then by practice of concentration, do thou seek to reach Me.

Once a man was having a coversation with a visitor when suddenly his dog started to lick his face. The visitor quickly denounced the action. From then on the owner gave the dog a hit everytime he tried to do this act. The animal was quick to learn.

Unwanted desires are like the wretched dog. Constant thoughts on God and His glories can drive them away. .

12-10

**abhyāse 'py asamartho 'si
matkarmaparamo bhava
madarthamapi karmāni
kurvan siddhimavāpsyasi**

If thou failest even to carry out this practice, give thyself up to My service; thou wilt attain perfection if thou only perform actions for My sake.

Habits cannot be easily changed but they can be pointed to God realization. A talkative person can speak about the glories of God all the time and a physically active individual can perform service to humanity instead of engaging in bondage causing activities.

Devotees divine traits (12-13 to 12-20)

12-13

**adveshtā sarvabhutānām
maitrah karuna eva ca
nirmamo nirahamkārah
samaduhkha-sukhah kshami**

12-14

**samtushtah satatam yogi
yatātmā dridhanishcayah
mayyarpita-mano-buddhir
yo madbhaktah sa me priyah**

He who bears no enmity towards any form of life, is friendly towards all, generous, free from feelings of possessiveness and arrogance, is not swayed by either intoxicated euphoria during good days and revenge-seeking depression during bad days. He easily forgives and is ever contented, poised as he is in a state of harmony. Dedicated to and intent upon Me, he is firm in his principles and beliefs. Such an aspirant is indeed very dear to me.

God attaches all importance to devotion, discrimination and detachment from worldliness.

Hatred *– an aggressive feeling born out of ignorance that one is a separate entity from others.*

Friendly *– the act of relating with another without expecting anything in return.*

When others feeling is extended to and directed towards the seeking the welfare of others, it is **compassion**. *The spiritual person's duty is to help others, but if he claims ownership to the service it becomes* **egoism**. *This can stop his spiritual progress or even ruin it. In his effort to render service an aspirant has to be prepared to take abuse and lose his possessions yet remain even minded, forbearing and tolerant. The yogi has gained the clarity, contentment and bliss in his newfound life. For no reason, should he sway in matters of spirituality as he runs the risks of losing this feeling. (12-13 & 12-14)*

12-15   *yasmām no 'dvijate loko*
                                   lokān no 'dvijate ca yaḥ
                                   harshāmarshabhayodvegair
                                   mukto yaḥ sa ca me priyaḥ

Such a one who does not offer provocation to the world and who is not provoked by the world, who is free from elation, envy, anxiety and fear, is dear to Me.

The surgeon operates on a patient for his or her betterment, a teacher disciplines a student as a part of his duty, a devotee in like manner renders service to humanity at large for its well-being. In return the devotee may receive harsh words or bad treatment but is not affected by them, instead the devotee sees these adverse acts as blessings from the Lord. Struggle is viewed as the Lord's grace (Prahlad).

A mind that will cherish joy will also disdain sorrow. Anger is the feeling when the desired result is not attained. Envy is the craving for something that has been achieved by another. Both these states are normal for mundane man but the devotee's mind is free from them.

Fear and also anxiety cause weakness and disturbance to the individual. They cause ceaseless sensations. But the devotee who sees all these as the dispensations of the Lord is dear to Him.

12-16

> *anapekshah shucirdaksha*
> *udāsino gatavyathah*
> *sarvārambhaparityāgi*
> *yo madbhaktah sa me priyah*

A devotee who expects nothing, is pure, efficient, impartial, undisturbed and has renounced attachment to all action, is dear to Me.

12-17

> *yo na hrishyati na dveshti*
> *na shocati na kānkshati*
> *shubhāshubha-parityāgi*
> *bhaktimān yah sa me priyah*

A devotee who neither rejoices nor hates, neither grieves nor hankers and who remains unmoved by good or evil, is dear to Me.

12-18

> *samah shatrau ca mitre ca*
> *tathā mānāpamānayoh*
> *shitoshnasukhaduhkheshu*
> *samah sangavivarjitah*

He who is alike to foe and friend, to good and evil in cold and heat, pleasure and pain and is free from detachment.

12-19

> *tulyanindāstutir mauni*
> *santushto yena kenacit*
> *aniketah sthiramatir*
> *bhaktimān me priyo narah*

He who holds equal blame or praise, who is silent (restrained in speech), and content with anything (that comes), who has no fixed abode and is firm in mind, is devoted and dear to Me.

The sun shines continuously but because the earth is rotating, we experience night and day. The devotee likewise being one pointed has no time to decide who is friend and who is foe. The devotee's mind and lifestyle is like an open book and the laws of the land are naturally observed. But the laws of God helps him to move steadily God ward. The items mentioned in these slokas are for the mundane man. (12-8 & 12-9)

12-20   *ye tu dharmāmritam idām*
                   yathoktam paryupāsate
                   sraddhadhānā matparamā
                   bhaktās te 'tiva me priyāh

Endowed with faith and solely devoted to me, those who pursue this immortal Dharma as set forth above, are devotees who are extremely dear to me.

Prem bhakti is when the devotee gives himself over to the Lord completely. He has gained inward spiritual strength, faith, contentment. Inward spiritual strength from pilgrimages and rituals and does not look for anything outside.

14-26   **mām ca yo 'vyabhicārena**
                   bhaktiyogena sevate
                   sa gunān samatityai 'tān
                   brahmabhuyāya kalpate

He who worships Me with unfaltering love transcends the gunas and becomes fit to attain oneness with the Brahman.

The devotee worships God with form and through the grace of the Lord realizes Him without form.

When devotion and knowledge gets harmonized, liberation ensues.

15-19   **yo mām evam asammudho**
                   jānāti purushottamam
                   sa sarvavid bhajati mām
                   sarvabhāvena bhārata

O Bharata (Arjuna), the un-deluded person who thus knows Me as the Supreme Person knows all that can be known. Therefore he worships Me with his whole being.

The undiluted ones see God in all of creation. His life's goal is to remove the delusion that has enveloped the Jivatman, to set it free and thereby allow it to merge into the Paramatman. In the end, the Gunas (Prakriti) get surrendered to God with form.

18-54
brahmabhutah prasannātmā
na shocati na kānkshati
samah sarveshu bhuteshu
madbhaktim labhate parām

Being one with Brahman, with tranquillity in mind, neither grieving nor craving, regarding all beings alike, he attains Supreme devotion unto Me.

Knowledge and devotion are not different. A mother loves her baby because the bond is there, knowing they are the same. The devotee is constantly performing the services of the Lord with devotion. The Lord reciprocates with the grace of knowledge that He exists in all of creation. The more one understands the scriptures his love for God increases.

18-55
bhaktyā mām abhijānāti
yāvān yashcā 'smi tattvatah
tato mām tattvato jnātvā
vishate tadanantaram

Through such devotion he comes to know Me, how much I am and in all My reality and principles of My being and having known Me in truth, he forthwith enters into Me (Purushottama).

After continuous faithful and devoted services to the Lord, one becomes a direct instrument in His hands and a helper in the maintenance of the Cosmic functions. The disciple allows himself to understand the ways of the Lord. In the end, the Lord accepts him as his own and the two merge.

18-57
cetasā sarvakarmāni
mayi samnyasya matparah
buddhiyogam upāshritya
maccittah satatam bhava

Giving up in thy conscious mind all thy actions into Me, devoting all of thyself to Me, resorting to yoga of the will and intelligence, be always one in heart and consciousness with Me.

The question that man asks is "If you receive the vision of God, what will you ask of Him?" the answer must be "I want to be united with you." Performing philanthropic activities are necessary for God realization but when God realization is attained, they are no longer needed.

To understand that the only undertaking of the Jivatman is to become united with the Cosmic Consciousness is Buddhiyoga. As an office bearer in the administration of a Govt. assumes and discharges his entrusted duties faithfully, in the same manner the aspirant ought to perform deeds to free himself from worldly ties and seek self-realization. This also is Buddhiyoga. Sant Tukaram at the time of ascending to heaven asked his wife to join him. She replied "I have to tend to the home and the cows". He ascended leaving her behind.

18-65   **manmanā bhava madbhakto**
                madyāji mām namashuru
                mamevai 'shyasi satyam te
                pratijāne priyo 'si me

Become My-minded, My lover and adorer, a sacrificer to Me. Bow thyself to Me, to Me thou shalt come; this is My pledge and promise to thee, for dear art thou to Me.

The purpose of Sri Krishna's incarnation is to reveal the truth of His relationship with the embodied soul (Jivatman). Just like the sun can only radiate its rays, the various schools of thoughts discuss the relationship of the individual souls with the Cosmic Soul and in the end the realization downs that these two are the same and the goal of life.

It is the nature of the mind to seek pleasant and enjoyable things that are counter-productive towards self-realization. When the love for God overshadows love for worldly possessions then the Lord is obligated to reciprocate likewise (Bhakta Prahlad).

18-67   **idam te nā 'tapaskāya**
                nā 'bhaktāya kadācana
                na cāshushrushave vācyam
                na ca mām yo 'bhyasuyati

Never speak of this to anyone who does not lead an austere life, who is lacking in devotion and is unwilling to hear nor to one who bears malice towards Me.

The Lord is saying here that Bhagavad-Gita will not benefit people who are indisciplined or who lead a life without austerity. Life without austerity is incomplete for spiritual progress. As such the Gita is of no benefit. If someone is not interested in the Gita, then it should not be preached to him.

18-68   **ya idam paramam guhyam**
                      madbhakteshvabhidhāsyati
                      bhaktim mayi parām kritvā
                      mām evai 'shyaty asamshayah

But he who is devoted to Me and teaches this supreme truth to My devotees in the spirit of worship shall certainly come to Me.

Imparting the knowledge and wisdom to others is a sure means to intellectual clarity. Teaching is a sure way of learning and is better than studying alone. One who can expound the Geeta should not assume the role of a master but only an instrument in the hands of the Lord. The role of a master fosters individuality (egoism) while that of a servant promotes devotion. The propagation of spiritual service is a sure means to access divinity. God, the scriptures and the true devotee are all one and the same.

Please read the slokas from "God's Grace" - Page 88 as they also pertain to this section.

Selfless service and duty

Key to selfless service

2-47
karmāny eva 'dhikāraste
mā phaleshu kadācana
mā karmaphalahetur bhur
mā te sango 'stv akarmani

Thou hast a right to action only, not to the fruit thereof. Thou shouldst not be guided by a consideration of the fruits of action nor shouldst thou feel drawn towards inaction.

Live in the world but don't let the word live in you. All actions are caused by one trying to gain something or trying to ward off something. Let the individual do what is good for him and not what he likes.

2-48
yogasthah kuru karmāni
sangam tyaktvā dhananjaya
siddyasiddhyoh samo bhutvā
samatvam yoga ucyate

O Dhananjaya (Arjuna), do thy work remaining steadfast in Yoga, giving up all hankering for the fruits of action, holding both success and failure alike. This spirit of equivalence is called Yoga.

A maid sevant shows sincere and total love for her masters children and property knowing that when she leaves the premise, that relationship is also left behind. Likewise, perform that which is required in your station in life knowing that one day it will all end.

2-49
durena hy avaram karma
buddhiyogād dhananjaya
buddhau sharanam anviccha
kripanāh phalahetavah

O Dhananjaya (Arjuna), action motivated by fruits of action is inferior to action done for the sake of action. So you should take resort to this spirit. Those who hanker for the fruits of action are objects of pity.

The Sadhaka should assume the role of a giver and never that of a grabber. As the ditches and lakes always get refilled the coffers of the devotee gets bigger and bigger.

2-50
**buddhiyukto jahāti 'ha
ubhe sukritadushkrite
tasmād yogāya yujyasva
yogah karmasu kaushalam**

The man who has attained the spirit of equivalence casts away both good and evil. Hence perform Yoga. Yoga is skill in action.

It is equanimity of mind that a doctor displays at the time of an operation. If the patient dies or is cured, he is not affected as he has performed his duty. However, if a close relation were to seek his service in a life or death situation he will have to refuse and seek the help of another doctor because attachment will prevent him from doing his duty efficiently. Good or bad karma perpetuates the cycle of birth and death. But the wise people like Bhishma overcame all Karma. He fought for the wicked Duryodhana valiantly but was never attached.

2-51
**karmajam buddhiyuktā hi
phalam tyaktvā manishinah
janmabandha vinirmuktāh
padam gacchanty anāmayam**

The wise who can attain to the spirit of equivalence renounces the fruits of their action and are set free from the bondage of birth. They reach a state of utter blissfulness.

Converting evil into good is a sign of greatness. With their lives, the great ones have assured themselves liberation by this science.

Knowledge and action compliment each other.

3-3
**sri bhagavān uvāca
loke 'smin dvividhā nisthā
putā proktā mayā 'nagha
jnānayogena sāmkhyānām
karmayogena yoginām**

The Lord said:O Thou Pure Soul, in the world, as I have already said, there are two courses of spiritual discipline, the samkhyas follow the path of knowledge and the yogis follow the path of action.

The Lord created the world as part of his playtime. He also created the paths for His creation to reunite with Him. Knowledge (discrimination and detachment) is the way of the introvert and detached actions the way of the extrovert, both leads to perfection or God realization.

3-5   **na hi kascit kshanam api
                jātu tisthaty akarmakrit
                kāryate hy avashah karma
                sarvah prakritijair gunaih**

Nobody can even take a moment off without doing work; for everybody is impelled to act in spite of himself by natural impulses.

Creation in its entirety is kinetic energy or moving energy. From the tiny atom to the vast universe, there are ceaseless actions caused by the gunas. It is a misconception that one can cease from action as breathing, sleeping, beating of the heart etc., continuous actions or karma. Until we master good action we are slaves of nature. Then when we do master it we fuse into Brahman or the action less plane.

3-6   **karmendriyāni samyamya
                ya āste manasā smaran
                indriyārthān vimudhātmā
                mithyācārah sa ucyate**

The self-deluded fool who remains holding his organs in check, but all the same dwells in his mind on the objects of sense, is called a hypocrite.

Sin and virtue accrue based on the state of the mind and not from bridling the senses. If the Sadhaka sits in the meditative pose but the mind drifts without sincere efforts to sublimate it then this is hypocrisy. Two friends decided to go out. One to the place of pleasure and the other to the place of worship. Their minds were on the other. The one that went to the worship place received blessings as his mind was on God.

3-7
yas tv indriyāni manasā
niyamyā 'rabhate 'rjuna
karmendriyaih karmayogam
asaktah sa vishishyate

The best of man is he, O Arjuna, who holding his senses in check by the power of mind and being free from attachment, addresses his organs of action to the path of action.

If the mind is made to constantly perform services thinking that it is for the Lord, then it will only be fixed on the Lord. However, if the mind it is allowed to follow the desire-laden senses, it will drag the individual through the roads of sensuality. The senses are like a poisonous snake. If the senses are curbed they can not serve their purposes but if they are sublimated, they will then take individual to liberation. (Story of the snake by the way side)

The wheel of life(14,15,16)

3-14
annād bhavanti bhutāni
parjanyād annasambhavah
yajnād bhavati parjanyo
yajnah karmasamudbhavah

From food comes the creatures, from rain comes the food, from sacrifice comes rain and sacrifice comes from action

The performance of the fire sacrifice has two benefits. The burning of the specially selected herbs and roots etc. acts, as a cleansing agent for the air and at the same time carbon dioxide is produced, beneficial for plants. The second is that on the mental plain a subtle force is released which induces rainfall.

3-15
karma brahmodbhavam viddhi
brahmā 'ksharasamudbhavam
tasmāt sarvagatam brahma
nityam yajne pratisthitam

Know this that action derives from the Vedas (Brahma), the Vedas derive from the Imperishable One. Hence the all-pervading Brahma is ever enshrined at the place of sacrifice.

When Karma or duty is performed perfectly and with the right motive, it becomes sacrifice. When the inhabitants of the universe take to sacrifice then the universe becomes elated and becomes a heavenly place.

3-16   ***evam pravartitam cakram***
                             nā 'nuvartayati 'ha yah
                             aghāyur indriyārāmo
                             mogham pārtha sa jivati

He who does not follow the wheel thus set turning round and round is a sensualist and lives a vile life. O Pārtha, he lives his life to no purpose.

The wheel of nature is set-up by the Lord for nursing, training, disciplining and elevating all beings at varying levels of existence. If a person does not perform his or her inherent duties, then he becomes a burden or dead weight to society. He causes disharmony in his own little way to the progress of self-realization and universal emancipation.

What a spiritual aspirant ought to do

3-20   ***karmanai 'va hi samsiddhim***
                             āsthitā janakādayah
                             lokasamgraham evā 'pi
                             sampasyan kartum arhasi

Janaka and others indeed achieved perfection by action,You also should perform action so as to set an example for the masses to follow.

3-21   ***yad-yad ācarati sresthas***
                             tat-tad eve 'taro janah
                             sa yat pramānam kurute
                             lokas tad anuvartate

Whatever a great man does is followed by others; people go by the example he sets up.

In public interest a person of eminence has therefore to put forth his best. Slighting or allowing godly gifts go to waste, amounts to slighting God Himself.

A man once took his son to the doctor. The doctor told the man to return the next day for the result. Upon returning the doctor adviced that the boy should not eat sweet. He continued to say that if he had told him the day before he would have been accused of being selfish as a bowl of candy was sitting on the table.

3-22
na me pārthā 'sti kartavyam
trisu lokesu kimcana
nā 'navāptam avāptavyam
varta eva ca karmani

There is nought in the three worlds, O Partha, that has not been done by Me, nor anything unattained that might be attained; still I engage in action.

Sri Krishna's role in the Mahabharata was far more than those of all the other characters put together. His duty was to maintain orderliness and precision for the maintenance of his creation.

3-23
yadi hy aham na varteyam
jātu karmany atandritah
mama vartmā 'nuvartante
manusyāh pārtha sarvasah

If ever I did not engage in work relentless, O Partha, men would in every respect follow My path.

Idleness, procastination and likes and dislikes to duty are readily caught by the ordinary man. The enlightened souls cannot afford to create doubts in the minds of the masses.

3-24
utsideyur ime lokā
na kuryām karma ced aham
samkarasya ca kartā
syām upahanyām imāh prajāh

These worlds would perish if I did not do action; I should be the cause of confusion of species and I should destroy these beings.

Perfomance of duty causes evolution to higher life and spirituality. The individual without sense of duty becomes a burden to society. He is worse than the dead. God is continuously at work to keep his creation moving towards salvation.

3-34

> *indriyasye 'ndriyasyā 'rthe*
> *rāgadvesau vyavasthitau*
> *tayor na vasam āgacchet*
> *tau hy asya paripanthinau*

In the very nature of things, senses are either attracted to or repelled by their objects. Thou shouldst not be swayed by such feelings. These are the enemies of man or stumbling blocks in the path of perfection.

The senses are mere instruments in the hands of Buddhi or understanding. They get attached to the objects when they are pleasant and repulsed by unpleasant things. These pairs of opposites govern the behavior of mundane man but for the God ward bound, they are pushed aside as he sees everything as temporary.

3-35

> *sreyān svadharmo vigunah*
> *paradharmāt svanusthitāt*
> *svadharme nidhanam sreyah*
> *paradharmo bhayāvahah*

One's own dharma, though imperfect, is better than the dharma of another well discharged. Better death in one's own dharma; the dharma of another is full of fear.

Arjuna's natural tendencies and training was to be a ruler and warrior. His fear and hatred to fight the great ones was causing him to leave his 'Swadharma'. If he would have retired as an ascetic his conscience would have destroyed his peace for ever. A true devotee of the Lord does not deviate from the path of salvation for no reason whatsoever.

4-12

> *kānkshantah karmanām siddhim*
> *yajanta iha devatāh*
> *kshipram hi mānushe loke*
> *siddhir bhavati karmajā*

Here those who desire success for their action, offer worship to Gods, for success from action comes quickly in this world.

Man can obtain quick results that are perceived by his senses but they are temporary. Self-realization, which is the grace of God or Guru, comes to those who ardently seek it.

4-14

na mām karmāni limpanti
na me karmaphale sprihā
iti mām yo 'bhijānāti
karmabhir na sa badhyate

I am not involved in action, I have no desire for the fruit of action. He who knows Me thus is not bound by action.

Emulation of the great souls is the way of the elite. Knowing that the world is and belongs to God the aspirant seeks to elevate himself where desires no longer haunt him. He no longer seeks to possess what others have as he realizes, this is the true cause of his separation from God.

4-15

evam jnātvā kritam karma
purvair api mumukshubhih
kuru karmai 'va tasmāt tvam
purvaih purvataram kritam

With this knowledge, the seekers of deliverance performed action in earlier times. Thou, too, perform the kind of action, which thy forerunners did in former ages.

The ignorant performs action for self-purification, while the wise works for the maintenance of the world.

The philosophy of action (4-16 to 4-22)

4-16

kim karma kim akarme 'ti
kavayo 'py atra mohitāh
tat te karma pravakshyami
yaj jnātvā mokshyase 'shubhāt

Even the wise feel confounded to understand what action or inaction is. So let me tell thee what action is. Thou wilt then be free from evil.

Toiling until one falls out from tiredness is not right action but performing the actions that will put an end to the cycle of birth and death are right actions.

4-17

karmano hy api boddhavyam
boddhavyam ca vikarmanah
akarmanas ca boddhavyam
gahanā karmano gatih

One has to understand about action as well about wrong (or improper) action and also about inaction. Thick and tangled is the way of action.

Follow the scriptures as to what is right and what is wrong.

4-18   **karmany akarma yah pashyed**
                 akarmani ca karma yah
                 sa buddhimān manushyeshu
                 sa yuktah kritsnakarmakrit

He who sees inaction in action and action in inaction, is wise among men. He is a yogi and universal doer of all works'.

The gunas or nature is the kinetic action or action state of God. And static or inaction state is Atman. Atman was, is and always will be forever permanent. The nature of God's creation is ever changing, in its process to become united again with Brahman or cosmic consciousness.

Because of the proximity, a ship in the vast ocean seems still, and the trees at the side of a moving train seems as if they are running backwards.

Out of ignorance one identifies him as being his body and then everything is action to his understanding. However, the spiritually advanced aspirant rightly identifies himself as the inactive ever-permanent Atman. He then realizes that all actions pertain to body, mind and intellect. The realized souls have arrived at their destination by saying "I am that." Inwardly they are action less but outwardly they purposely engage their minds and senses in ceaseless action to educate the masses of what is real and what is unreal. Once the differentiation is realized it is never lost again whereas the mundane man only knows about the physical body.

Arjuna wanted to go to the forest and become an ascetic. This would have been of no use, as his mind would have been made restless and less peaceful than if he were to have engaged himself in the great Mahabharata.

Lord Krishna, the symbol of inaction personified, stood solid as a rock. While his left hand was in action ready to control the steeds, his right hand was in chinamudra (the symbol of knowledge imparting). A yogi is he whose head is always in solitude and whose hands are in society. He thus accrues permanent vacation in the mundane world.

4-19   *yasya sarve samārambhāh*
                         kāmasamkalpavarjitāh
                         jnānāgnidagdhakarmānam
                         tam āhuh panditam budhāh

The wise call that man a sage, all of whose efforts are devoid of desire and whose ego is burnt up by the fire of wisdom.

It is but natural that the aspirant always appears busy because he has permanently become an instrument in the hands of the Lord. The Lord appropriately puts him in the duties that are conducive to his liberation and at the same time are conducive to the emancipation of society. He willingly accepts what comes his way. He neither designs nor creates but yet is always in peace.

4-20   *tyaktvā karmaphalāsangam*
                         nityatripto nirāsrayah
                         karmany abhipravritto 'pi
                         nai 'va kimchit karoti sah

Having given up attachment to the fruit of action, ever content, free from dependence, he does nothing though deep in action.

Action and inaction are states of the mind. Because of the relationship that has developed between the Lord and his disciple, instruction through intuition is the guiding force as to what is action and what is inaction. Situations and people are merely the stage; the disciple carries out the Lord's instructions with joy not depending on any one.

Vyasadev once ate his bellyfull and then asked the river Jamuna to stop flowing if it is true that he has maintained his fasting. The river did stop flowing, and the Gopies then crossed. By eating he only appeased the deity residing in the body but his mind was anchored to Sri Krishna.

4-21   *nirāshir yatacittātmā*
                         tyaktasarva parigrahah
                         shāriram kevalam karma
                         kurvan nā 'pnoti kilbisham

Being free from desire, with his mind and senses under control, renouncing all worldly goods, acting only through the body, he is not tainted by sin.

Sin is that karma which retards the moral and spiritual growth of man. Sin is born of desires. The Yogi desires naught. His needs are reduced to bare bodily requirements. He does not accumulate anything and avoids receiving gifts that will put him under obligation.

4-22   *yadricchā lābha samtushto*
                            dvandvātito vimatsarah
                            samah siddhāv asiddhau ca
                            kritvā 'pi na nibadhyate

He who remains content with whatever falls to his lot, is free from envy, has soared beyond all pairs of opposites (like joy and grief), remains steadfast alike in success and failure, and though performing actions, is not subject to bondage.

God provides for those who surrender to Him. The Lord in turn, provides for the needs of His disciple, which are food and a few pieces of clothing. The disciple is happy to see the prosperity of all and never is he envious. He works with the philosophy that first feed and clothes the hungry and poor and then tell him about God.

Varities of sacrifice (4-23 to 4-33)

4-23   *gatasamgasya muktasya*
                            jnānāvasthitacetasah
                            yajnāyā 'caratah karma
                            samagram praviliyate

He whose attachment has disappeared, whose mind rests secure in knowledge and who works in the spirit of sacrifice - all his actions dissolve away.

Seek the protection of God first by equipping yourself with self-knowledge before you acquire wealth for it will be the cause of your bondage.

4-27   *sarvāni 'ndriyakarmāni*
                            prānakarmāni cā 'pare
                            ātma-samyama-yogāgnau
                            juhvati jnānadipite

Others again offer all the activities of their senses and also of their vital force into the flame of self-discipline, kindled   by wisdom.

When the mind is identified with Ataman it is referred to as the fire of self-control. It creates the link between the outside world and the Atman but when it merges with Atman, all the actions of the senses and life-energy become sanctified.

4-32   ***evam bahuvidhā yajnā***
             vitatā brahmano mukhe
             karmajān viddhi tān sarvān
             evam jnātvā vimokkshyase

Many such forms of sacrifice have been set forth in detail through the lips of Brahman. Know this that all these derive from action.Knowing thus, thou shalt be set free.

Veda is the study of the functions of nature and nature is the embodiment of Karma. To convert karma into sacrifice is to confirm to the sacred plan of nature or to seek liberation.

4-33   ***sreyān dravyamayād yajnāj***
             jnānayajnāh paramtapa
             sarvam karmā 'khilam pārtha
             jnāne parisamāpyate

O Scourge of Foes, yajna in the form of knowledge is superior to yajna performed with material things. Know thou this, O Partha, that all actions in their totality, find their culmination and completeness, in knowledge of the Divine.

Accumulation of wealth, of more than what is actually required, causes anxiety and draws the individual away from the acquisition of intelligence. "It is easier for a camel to pass through the eye of a needle than a rich man to enter into heaven." A balance of wealth and knowledge leads to wisdom is the knowledge of what is real and what is unreal.

Selfless action is renunciation

(5-1 to 5-14 see renunciation - Page 217)

8-3   *sri bhagavān uvāca*
                         aksharambrahma paramam
                         svābhāvo 'dhyātmam ucyate
                         bhutabhāvodbhavakaro
                         visargah karmasamjnitah

The Lord said:Brahman is the Supreme, Imperishable Being (Absolute). It
is called adhyātma when the Brahman manifests itself in individual souls.
And the sacrifices released in the creative forces of the universe are known
as Karma.

*Karma is the sum total of all actions that cause man's creation, his growth and
prosperity. Absolute reality and Brahman is beyond time, space and causation,
the universe or the swabhava. Swabhava means property, duty and merit of a
person. The Swabhava of the absolute reality of the God before creation is to
project itself as the multitude of all individual souls.*

9-9   *na ca mām tāni karmāni*
                         nibadhnanti dhananjaya
                         udāsinavad āsinam
                         asaktam teshu karmasu

O Dhananjaya (Winner of wealth, Arjuna), those actions cannot bind Me,
for I remain unconcerned, unattached to those actions.

*Nature is the spouse of Isvara. Isvara gives the power and Nature the action.
The Lord is like the screen in a movie theatre. All the actions take place on him
but yet He is not affected. The disciple likewise lives in the world physically,
but is anchored in Brahman.*

9-12   *moghāsha moghkarmāno*
                         moghajnānā vicetasah
                         rākhsasim āsurim cai 'va
                         praktitim mohinim sritāh

These senseless persons have been overwhelmed by the nature of fiends and demons and are suffering thus from delusions. Vain are their aspirations, their actions and their knowledge.

They whose hopes, activities and understanding are attracted only to sense pleasures are called -

Rakshasas – *rajasic nature is predominant*
Asursas – *tamasic nature is predominant*

9-27   ***yat karoshi yad ashnāsi***
                          yaj juhosi dadasi yat
                          yat tapssyasi kaunteya
                          tat kurusva madarpanam

O Son of Kunti (Arjuna), whatever thou doest, eatest or giveth, whatever thou offerest as sacrifice and whatever austerities thou performest, do that as an offering unto Me.

Sri Ramakrishna usually prayed to Mother Kali "My doings are all your doings, not I, not I but you". At Bharat Sevashram Sangha surrender, detachment and celibacy are necessary for spiritual progress. These are all aids to be better able to dedicate one's life to serving society. However, serving society and these austerities are just means to self-realization and not the goal.

9-28   ***shubhāshubhaphalair evam***
                          mokshyase karmabandhanaih
                          sannyāsayogayuktātmā
                          vimukto mām upaishyasi

It thou offerest all actions unto Me, thou shalt free yourself from both the good and evil effects of thy actions. With thy mind firmly planted in renunciation, liberated thou shalt come unto Me.

11-55   ***matkarmakrin matparamo***
                          madbhaktah sangavarjitah
                          nirvairah sarvabhuteshu
                          yah sa mām eti pāndava

O Pandava (Arjuna), he who works for Me, regards Me as his goal, worships Me, unattached, and bears enmity to none, comes to Me.

Mind does not cling to two things at the same time. Devotion to the Lord reduces attachment to the world and eventually complete detachment is the result. The love for the Lord must be one-pointed and then all entrapments of the world will vanish

The worship of saguna Brahman (6,10,11)

12-6   *ye tu sarvāni karmāni*
                        mayi samnyasya matparāh
                        ananyenai 'va yogena
                        mām dhyāyanta upāsate

But those who surrendering all their actions to Me, meditate on Me and worship Me with single-hearted devotion and whose thoughts are centred on Me, O Pārtha (Arjuna), I rescue these dedicated devotees ere long from the ocean of mortal existence.

12-10   *abhyāse 'py asamartho 'si*
                        matkarmaparamo bhava
                        madarthamapi karmāni
                        kurvan siddhimavāpsyasi

It thou failest even to carry out this practice, give thyself up to My service; thou wilt attain perfection if thou only perform actions for My sake.

Habits cannot be easily changed but they can be pointed to God realization. A talkative person can speak about the glories of God all the time and a physically active individual can perform service to humanity instead of engaging in bondage causing activities.

12-11   *athaitad apy ashakto 'si*
                        kartum madyogam āshritah
                        sarvakarmaphalatyāgam
                        tatah kuru yatātmavān

If thou failest even in this, then take refuge in Me, renounce the fruit of all actions, with thy self controll.

Union with God is a systematic process. Every individual's inborn nature forces him to perform actions.

The following are what should be told to the masses -
1) *Controlled life will make his earnings last longer.*
2) *More earning will come to him as his belief in God increases.*

Offering a portion of his earnings to God's children will cause his wealth to multiply.

In this manner, the individual will become a devotee, thereby unconsciously moving onto the path of realization.

13-30
prakrityai 'va ca karmāni
kriyamānāni sarvashah
yah pashyati tathātmānam
akartāram sa pashyati

He who sees that all actions are done by prakriti (nature) and that the self is not the doer, he sees truly.

The Jnani more than anyone else is full of activities because of his duty to be the perfect example. However, he knows his true identity is action less. No person can stay action less so long as he is in the body. We have to admire God in his action less state and also in His ever-active manifested state.

13-31
anāditvān nirgunatvāt
paramātmā 'yam avyayah
sharirastho 'pi kaunteya
na karoti na lipyate

O Son of Kunti (Arjuna), being without beginning and without attributes (Gunas), the Supreme Self is immutable and though He dwells in the body, He performs no action nor is affected by the fruits of action.

Brahman is the first or supreme original consciousness. Creation of Prakriti came afterwards at the will and the dominance of Brahman. Prakriti is ever active because of the Gunas. Prakriti or the active part of God cannot affect his inactive static aspect or un-manifested state. It was, is or will be perfection.

14-15
rajasi pralayam gatvā
karmasangishu jāyate
tathā pralinas tamasi
mudhayonishu jāyate

He who dies while rajas predominate will be born among those attached to action and if he departs if tamas predominates he will be born in the womb of stupid creatures.

The passionate (rajasic) person lives in excitement, sorrow and desires. In his rebirth he is given to excessive activity. The lazy (tamasika) man dies in unconsciousness state and takes rebirth as subhuman.

14-16   ***karmanah sukritasyā 'huh***
                    sāttvikam nirmalam phalam
                    rajasas tu phalam dukhham
                    ajnānam tamasah phalam

It is said that the fruit of good action, stemming from sattva guna, is pure bliss, while the fruit from raja guna is pain and that from tama guna is ignorance.

The tamasika person is either inactive or involved in wicked deeds.

The rajasic individual is prosperous but because of his incessant actions he gets himself in misery. However these miseries serve as training ground for knowing right duties .

The sattvika person is ever brilliant and pure and this is evident in his disposition.

17-27   ***yajne tapasi dāne ca***
                    sthitih sad iti co 'cyate
                    karma caiva tadarthiyam
                    sa ity evābhidhiyate

Steadfastness in sacrifice, austerity and gift is also called Sat; so any action dedicated towards these ends is called Sat.

If the intent is good, but by ignorance the method is incorrect then by uttering 'SAT', it gets purified. When SAT is uttered, it creates and draws ones mind to think of the reality of God in his state before creation. Sacrifice, austerity and gifts are done to purify the individual, thereby taking him a step closer to Godhood. Any mistake(s) made in this, means that the end "can be set right" by uttering 'SAT'.

18-7
niyatasya tu sannyāsaḥ
karmano no 'papadyate
mohāt tasya parityāgas
tāmasaḥ parikirtitaḥ

It is not proper to renounce the duty, which has been ordained. The abandonment of such a duty, through delusion, is said to be tamasic in nature.

18-8
duḥkham ity eva yat karma
kāyakleshabhayāt tyajet
sa kritvā rājasam tyāgam
nai va tyāgaphalam labhet

If he abstains from action because it is painful or from fear of physical discomfort, his renunciation is rājasic in nature. He does not derive any benefit from such relinquishment.

After viewing the world as a place of troubles and difficulties some take to sanyasa life. This escapist act to avoid body pain and mental agony is of no use. Instead the individual becomes a parasite to society, When Arjuna thought of retreating to the forest as a sanyasin and abandon his duties as a Kshatriya Lord Krishna was prompted to deliver the message of Geeta.

Components of action(18-13 to 18-16)

18-13
pancai 'mani mahābāho
kāranāni nibodha me
sāmkhye kritānte proktāni
siddhaye sarvakarmanām

O Mighty-armed One (Arjuna), learn from Me the five factors which generate action according to the Sāmkhya doctrine.

The inherent forces of nature are the active or lower nature of God. The soul of man coexists in the field of action. When it cannot distinguish itself from the forces of nature then the five factors of actions become the dominant rulers of destiny. The forces of nature at the same time become the training ground for the soul to educate itself about the Supreme Self.

18-14   *adhishthānam tathā kartā*
                         karanam ca prithagvidham
                         vividhās ca prithak ceshtā
                         daivam caivātra pancamam

The five causes of action are the body, the agent, the various senses, the different and manifold functions, and Providence, is the fifth.

The five factors of actions are -
    Body *-experiencing and understanding*
    Ego *– recording the experiences*
    Senses *- knowing and acting*
    Breathing *- the living force*
    Individual soul *– or deity-controlling force*

The workings of a motorcar can be compared to these five factors.
    Factory *– place of existence*
    Owner *- agent*
    Wheel and drive *- senses*
    Petrol *- life energy*
    Driver *- presiding deity*

18-15   *shariravānmanobhir yat*
                         karma prārabhate narah
                         nyāyyam vā viparitam vā
                         pancai 'te tasya hetavah

These are the five causes of action, good or bad, which a man performs with the aid of his body, speech and mind.

The human body, just like a car, can be used for various purposes, good or bad. It can be made into a temple or it can be used to perform diabolic acts. The activities that emanate from the body are thoughts, words and deeds. The origin of all words and deeds are thoughts, either criminal or pious.

18-16   *tatrai 'vam sati kartāram*
                         ātmānam kevalam tu yah
                         pashyaty akritabuddhitvān
                         na sa pashyati durmatih

In spite of this being the case, the person, who because of his perverted mind and imperfect judgement, views the Absolute Self as the agent, does not see the truth at all.

The parts of a car come from the earth or the five elements. The car runs on the earth but the earth does not control it. The relationship of the car to the earth is the same as the Paramatman to the individual soul. The soul or the sixth sense is subject to change; it has to merge with the immovable, full and perfect Paramatman. Although, air and space is subtle, space is immovable. Air exists in it. Individual souls have the same relationship with the all-pervading soul.

18-17
> *yasya nā 'hamkrito bhāvo*
> *bhuddhir yasya na lipyate*
> *hatvā 'pi sa imāmllokān*
> *na hanti na nibadhyate*

He who is free from ego, whose understanding is unaffected, though he may slay these people, is no slayer nor shall action bind him.

As one comes closer to the Cosmic Conscious state, loosing his body becomes less and less fearful. Bhishma while lying on the bed of arrows was delivering to Veda Vyasa and others, the message of Hindu dharma. He waited many days for the sun to resume the bright path, before leaving his body. Arjuna's so called killing Bhishma had no doer-ship effect on him as Bhishma told him how he could be killed or conquered

The three gunas – the cause of action (18-18 to 18-40)

18-18
> *jnānam jneyam parijnātā*
> *trividhā karmacodanā*
> *karanam karma karte 'ti*
> *trividhah karmasamgrahah*

Knowledge, knower and that which is known - these three motivate action. The instrument (senses), the object and the agent (doer) - these are the threefold basis of action.

Academic knowledge, object of knowledge as perceived by the senses, and the Jivatman the knower, comprises the triad of knowledge.

Action, the instrument and the objects make up the triad of karma or action. Governed by the triad, the mind, the speech and the body perform respective functions.

Instruments are two fold, internal and external. Mind, intellect and ego are internal. The body, tongue, eyes, ears and nose are the external organs of the organs of knowledge and action. The embodied soul is the subtle agent that incorporates action and knowledge for it's self-culture and evolution to the higher plane of cosmic consciousness.

18-19   ***jnānam karma ca kartā ca***
                   tridhai 'va gunabhedatah
                   procyate gunasamkhyāne
                   yathāvacchrinu tānyapi

Sāmkhya philosophy affirms that knowledge, action and the doer (agent) are of three kinds only, according to the guna, which predominates in each. Hear of them duly from Me.

Sankhya philosophy by sage Kapila is the authority on the three-nature of man, knowledge and action. The concept of action can be understood based on the competence of students namely, - first rate, mediocre and slow.

18-23   ***niyatam sangarahitam***
                   arāgadveshatah kritam
                   aphalaprepshunā karma
                   yat tat sāttvikam ucyate

An action, which is done from a sense of duty, without attachment, free from love or hate and with unconcern for the fruit, is said to be of the sattvic order.

Duty for duties sake is the essence of the sattvika persons. He discharges his duties incessantly with ease and excellence. His spiritual practice is not displayed for the public show but done in privacy.

18-24   ***yat tu kāmepsuna karma***
                   sāhamkārena vā punah
                   kriyate bahulāyāsam
                   tad rājasam udāhritam

But that action which is performed with painful effort, with longing for objects of desire or from a sense of egoism is said to be of rājasic order.

Desires are of two kinds, those that take the individual on the moral path or through self less service to humanity and those that further entangle him to earthly life. To be in the human body is blessed but the usage of it varies. If it be looked at as a thing of show, and used for pleasure it is egoistic, hence it is rajasika. Desires that cause excessive mental agony are a sign that action is not ones swabhava and is designated as rajasika.

18-25 **anubandham kshayam himsām**
anapekshya ca paurusham
mohād ārabhyate karma
yat tat tāmasam ucyate

The action, which is undertaken from delusion, without heed to ability, consequence, loss or injury to others, is said to be of the tāmasic order.

Misuse of money, wastage of time and energy are bad habits normal in the tamasika person. Ignorance of ability and being stupid in the name of simplicity is also tamasika.

18-26 **muktasango 'nahamvādi**
dhrityutsāhasamanvitah
siddhyasiddhyor nirvikārah
kartā sāttvica ucyate

The agent who is without desire or ego, who is endowed with perseverance and enthusiasm, is unaffected by success or failure is said to be of the sattvic order.

The aspirant, as an instrument in the hands of God surrenders all the fruits of his actions to the Lord. This kind of conviction removes all doubts and also creates the urge to constantly engage in service to humanity and in the glorification of the Lord. All mental agony and physical ailments become minimized.

18-27 **rāgi karmaphalaprepsur**
lubdho himsātmako 'shucih
harshashokānvitah kartā
rājasah parikirtitah

The agent who is swayed by passion, joy and sorrow, who seeks the fruit of action, is greedy, harmful and impure is said to be of the rājasic order.

Rajasika quality is to acquire what belongs to others by hook or crook. The rajasika persons are always, mentally planning and physically executing by force or cunningness, (just like a crow) to add to their belongings. They also seek constant enjoyment and brag of their acquisitions.

18-28   ***ayuktah prākritah stabdhah***
               satho naishkritiko 'lasah
               vishādi dirghasutri ca
               kartā tāmasa ucyate

The agent who is unstable, vulgar, arrogant, dishonest, malicious, indolent, procrastinating and is easily dejected belongs to the order of tamas.

Unsteady - one who is not anchored in religious life.

Vulgar —one who is craving for sensual pleasures and is childish.

Stubborn — one who lacks respect for the worthy

Deceitful — one who does not use his talents for good causes

Malicious —one who willfully creates hatred among people

Indolent —one who does not complete his prescribed duties.

Despondent —one who is mentally weak, depressive and full of dejection

Procrastination —one who leaves duties for the morrow

These tamasika men are like fishes they make no effort to escape the net of life while the rajasika have made efforts to escape and the sattvika have freed themselves and are well on their path to liberation.

Caste system-duty that leads to liberation (41 to 48)

18-41   ***brāhmana kshatriya vishām***
               sudrānām ca parantapa
               karmāni pravibhktāni
               svabhāvaprabhavair gunaih

O Chastiser of Foes (Arjuna), the duties of Brāhmanas, Kshatriyas, and Vaishyas as well as of Sudras have been prescribed according to the qualities (gunas) they inherit from nature (prakriti).

Swabhava - the tendencies of a person

Sanskaras - mental images that are left by actions. No two persons are alike. This is the plan of creation and sustenance. It is also the plan of the Lord for every created being to move up the ladder of evolution to the infinite state.

Human beings can be grouped into four categories or Varna dharma.

18-42   **shamo damastapah shaucam**
           kshāntir ārjavameva ca
           jnānam vijnānamāstikyam
           brahmakarma svabhāvajam

A Brāhmana's duties, born of his nature, are control of mind and senses, austerity, purity, forgiveness, simplicity, wisdom, realization and faith in God.

> **Serenity** - *peacefulness of mind emanating from realization*

> **Self-restraint** - *lack of irrational response due to sense control and self control;*

> **Austerity** - *control of body, mind and speech*

> **Purity** - *to be establish in the original state.*

> **Forgiveness** - *accommodating and non-retaliation to mistakes and taunting from others*

> **Uprightness** - *welfare of all through thoughts, words and deeds.*

> **Knowledge** - *belief in God and his creation and insight into the God realization.*

> **Realization** - *the differentiation between mundane and knowing that God is the only real*

All the thoughts, words and deeds are motivated by the realization that the life continues after death. The Brahmans possessions are just enough for his basic needs and his sojourn on earth is the like that of a pilgrim. His presence together with other Brahmans lifts society to spiritual heights.

18-43   **shauryam tejo dhritir dākshyam**
           yuddhe cā 'pyapalāyanam
           dānam ishvarabhāvash ca
           kshātram karma svabhāvajam

The duties of a Kshatriya, ordained by his nature, are prowess, vigour, steadfastness, skill, dauntlessness in battle, generosity and command over others.

The Kshatriya is the embodiment of duty and an ideal man. His duty is to put man's earthly life on the path to realization. In this process, he is not afraid to sacrifice his body for he will never accept a life of slavery. The enemy never intimidates the Kshatriya even if he is overpowered, for his firmness and resourcefulness takes him out of difficult situations. He may retreat out of tact but with the realization that at a later stage he will do the needful.

Generosity is the maximum distribution of one's wealth to the deserving masses for their welfare and prosperity. The Kshatriya ensures this. His mental makeup makes him a leader as he upholds the law of the land. He becomes the beacon light for others. Thus he is on the brink of becoming a Brahman.

18-44   ***krishi gaurakshya vānijyam***
              vaishyakarma svabhāvajam
              paricaryātmakam karma
              sudrasyā 'pi svabhāvajam

Cultivation, rearing of cattle and trade are the duties of a Vaishya born of his nature, while to serve is the natural duty of a Sudra.

Vaisyas create and distribute the wealth of society. They earn this wealth by creating industries and by becoming professionals.

The Sudras are the paid laborers who work for other classes. An office worker who is always under the supervision of another person is also considered Sudra. However, the Govt. workers, the personnel in the army are all Kshatriyas.

All societies of the world are made-up of this division of labor. They may not define it as such but based on the mentality and the means, a structured society functions best when each category is given the opportunity to excel in their abilities. For example in America the garbage collector, the policeman, the farmer and the school principal gets the same benefits and respect. However, if the mental makeup of an individual changes he can shift to another profession. Upward movement is natural.

The Brahmans can perform the duties of any other class but the sudra's mentality prevents him from discharging the functions of the higher group effectively.

However, anyone can rise to God-realization. Efficient execution of duty is the deciding factor and not the type of work.

In the human body the brain does the Brahmin's duty, the stomach the Vaishyas the heart the Kshatriya's and the limbs, the sudras' duties. The Lord, recognizes classes and also equates the four yogas accordingly. A sadhaka of Brahman tendencies will naturally take to the path of jnana yoga (knowledge), the Kshatriya to bhakti, the Vaishya and the Sudra to meditation.

18-45   **sve sve karmany abhiratah**
              samsiddhim labhate narah
              svakarmaniratah siddhim
              yathā vindati tacchrinu

When one follows his own duty devotedly, he attains perfection. Hear now how one, following one's duty devotedly, attains perfection.

The late Dr. Martin Luther King an African Civil Rights leader of America spoke, "if I am a street sweeper let me be the best one", President John F Kennedy said "Ask not what your country can do for you but what you can do for your country" and Gita's main message is "ask not what is your right but what is your duty". Execution of your duty is your key to liberation. Craving to do another's duty only creates disharmony and confusion.

18-46   **yatah pravrittir bhutānām**
              yena sarvam idam tatam
              svakarmanā tamabhyarcya
              siddhim vindati mānavah

Man attains perfection by doing his duty as an act of worship to God, who is the source of all beings and by Whom all this is pervaded.

Worshipping the Lord and performing ones duty must be interrelated. Wretched is he who sees them different as every being is an equal and important component of the cosmic plan. In the Vyadha Geeta a butcher gave advice to an ascetic. The butcher regarded his job as worship to the Lord, giving full expression and fulfilling his swadharma (natural tendencies) while making an honest living. He is a yogi who in thought, word and deed regards his earthly life as worship to God.

18-47   *shreyān svadharmo vigunah*
                 paradharmāt svanushthitāt
                 svabhāvaniyatam karma
                 kurvan nāpnoti kilbisham

A man's own natural duty, though executed imperfectly, is better than work, not naturally his own, even if that is well performed. When a man does his duty according to the law of his nature, he incurs no sin.

The purpose of the human birth is to elevate the soul to Godhood and not to secure a permanent abode on earth by amassing excess wealth. The latter causes a waste of precious time as he deviates form the path of realization. A yogi is he who achieves the maximum benefit with minimum effort. To stick to one's swadharma is to utilize the inherent qualities that have been acquired over births. To arbitrarily change ones duties because of likes and dislikes creates frustration and disharmony to Gods law. What is the goal of life? Self-realization, and universal, emancipation? said   Sri Pranavanandaji

18-48   **sahajam karma kaunteya**
                 sadosham api na tyajet
                 sarvārambhā hi doshena
                 dhumenā 'gnirivā 'vritāh

O Son of Kunti (Arjuna), no one should give up his natural work, even though he does it imperfectly (or even though it is attended with defect). For all action is tainted with imperfection as fire is clouded by smoke.

The yogi performs all actions with the motive of reaching Godhood. He follows his swadharma as he realizes this is the prescribed duty of God. The mundane man however is caught in the conflict of what is virtue and what is vice. Virtue is the act of doing more good than evil and vice is the opposite. No act is free from evil. Breathing causes the death of millions of microbes.

18-49   **asaktabuddhih sarvatra**
                 jitātmā vigatasprihah
                 naishkarmasiddhim paramām
                 sannyāsenā 'dhigacchati

He who is fully non-attached, self-controlled and devoid of desire, attains supreme perfection of naishkarmya through renunciation of the fruits of action.

A karma yogi or a sanyasin is constantly involved in activities. He does not have a permanent place of rest. Anyplace is his residence. As myriads of work come to him so they are dispersed in the same manner as water flows under a bridge. Ill feelings, good feelings, likes and dislikes, don't arise in his mind as he has reached the state of placidity due to his mastery over his original identity and his soul. Desires have been conquered through wisdom

18-56
**sarvakarmāny api sadā
kurvāno madvyapāshrayaḥ
matprasādād avāpnoti
shāshvatam padam avyayam**

Even though constantly performing all actions, taking refuge in Me, he attains through My grace the Eternal, Imperishable State.

Selfless service to humanity is a means to God realization. It is the sure way to attain the purified state and that is also a stepping-stone for union with Brahman. Selfless service of Karma yoga is when the Sadhaka gradually relinquishes the doer ship while serving humanity. He is the originator of the act. The mundane man feels weariness, exhaustion and frustration during work. The Sadhaka performs the same tasks with ease and comfort.

The water in a river has an individual identity but when it merges with the ocean it's flow is no longer distinct and separate. This has now become the duty of the ocean.

18-57
**cetasā sarvakarmāni
mayi samnyasya matparaḥ
buddhiyogam upāshritya
maccittaḥ satatam bhava**

Giving up in thy conscious mind all thy actions into Me, devoting all thyself to Me, resorting to yoga of the will and intelligence, be always one in heart and consciousness with Me. (Sri Aurobindo)

The question that man asks is "If you receive the vision of God, what will you ask of Him?" the answer must be "I want to be united with you." Performing philanthropic activities are necessary for God realization but when God realization is attained, they are no longer needed.

To understand that the only undertaking of the Jivatman is to become united with the Cosmic Consciousness is Buddhiyoga. As an office bearer in the administration of a Govt. assumes and discharges his entrusted duties faithfully, in the same manner the aspirant ought to perform deeds to free himself from worldly ties and seek self-realization. This also is Buddhiyoga.

18-60

svabhājena kaunteya
nibaddhah svena karmanā
kartum ne 'cchasi yan
mohāt karisyasy avaso 'pi tat

O Son of Kunti (Arjuna), that which from delusion, thou desirest not to do, thou shalt helplessly do that very thing, caught in the trammels of thy action, arising from thy own nature (swabhava).

The innate tendencies cannot be hidden. They become evident in words and deeds. To overcome them, is to act in tune with them. This will purify the individual thereby making him receptive for the grace of the Lord. Dreams are the reflections of an individual nature and they serve as a release of experiences during the day.

Knowledge and Wisdom

2-68
tasmād yasya mahābāho
nigrihitāni sarvashah
indriyāni 'ndriyārthebhyas
tasya prajnā pratisthitā

O Thou of Strong Arms, one whose senses have in all ways been withdrawn from their objects, have attained the state of serene wisdom.

The senses cannot be made to stand still. However, the attitude with which they are used determine the difference between sin and virtue. The eyes being the most dangerous should be trained to see the opposite sex as temples of God. Eating to maintain a fit body is virtue but to satisfy the tongue at every calling is sin. When all the senses become the slave of the individual then God will reveal Himself.

3-3
shri bhagavān uvāca
loke 'smin dvividhā nisthā
putā proktā mayā 'nagha
jnānayogena sāmkhyānām
karmayogena yoginām

The Blessed Lord said:O Thou Pure Soul, in the world, as I have already said, there are two courses of spiritual discipline, the sankhyas betaking themselves to the path of knowledge and the yogis betaking themselves to the path of action.

3-39
āvritam jnānam etena
jnānino nityavairinā
kāmarupena kaunteya
duspurenā 'nalena ca

Knowledge is enveloped, O Son of Kunti (Arjuna) by this insatiable fire of desire, the eternal foe of the wise.

Desires can never be satisfied by the enjoyment of the objects of desires. Desires grow more and more, just as fire blazes when fuel is thrown into it. Although the wise tries to keep it at bay it always finds a way to reappear.

3-40   *indriyāni mano budhir*
                           asyā 'dhisthānam ucyate
                           etair vimohayaty esha
                           jnānam āvritya dehinam

It is said that it has its seat in senses, mind and intellect. Enveloping our wisdom through these, it casts its spell on the embodied soul.

When desires take control, the disciple is dragged by the base habits of lust and greed. The soul is the only thing to know that desires are impossible to eliminate. In other words, if an alternative is not created then mundane life becomes the force of attraction and repulsion.

3-41   *tasmāt tvam indriyāny ādau*
                           niyamya bharatarshabha
                           pāpmānam prajahi by enam
                           jnānavijnāna-nāshanam

Hence, O Greatest of Bharatas, first restraining the senses,, slay this sinful desire which seeks to destroy knowledge and realization.

Anything that obstructs spiritual growth is maya or illusion.The right understanding of the scriptures is knowledge and intuition of God as consciousness, is realization.

4-19   *yasya sarve samārambhāh*
                           kāmasamkalpavarjitāh
                           jnānāgnidagdhakarmānam
                           tam āhuh panditam budhāh

The wise call that man a sage, all whose efforts are devoid of desire and whose ego is burnt up by the fire of wisdom.

It is but natural that the aspirant always appears busy because he has permanently become an instrument in the hands of the Lord. The Lord appropriately involves him in the duties that are conducive to his liberation and at the same time are conducive to societies' emancipation. He willingly accepts what comes his way. He neither designs nor creates but yet is always at peace.

4-27

sarvāni 'ndriyakarmāni
prānakarmāni cā 'pare
ātma-samyama-yogāgnau
juhvati jñānadipite

Others again offer all the activities of their senses and also of their vital force into the flame of self-discipline, kindled by wisdom.

When the mind is identified with Ataman it is referred to as the fire of self-control. It creates the link between the outside world and the Atman but when it merges with Atman, all the action of the senses and life-energy becomes sanctified.

4-28

dravyayajñās tapoyajñā
yogayajñās tathā 'pare
svādhyāya-jñānayajñas ca
yatayah samsitavratāh

Some offer as sacrifice their worldly goods or their austerities or their yogic practices, such as breath-control. Others chaste rigorous souls offer their study and scholarship of the holy text of the Vedas.

Man reforms himself through austerity and self-purification. Sincere and devotional offerings are replenished in manifold ways by the Lord. For example, he who preaches the Geeta receives the essence of it both academically and spiritually.

4-33

sreyān dravyamayād yajñāj
jñānayajñāh paramtapa
sarvam karmā 'khilam pārtha
jñāne parisamāpyate

O Scourge of Foes, yajna in the form of knowledge is superior to yajna performed with material things. Know thou this, O Pārtha, that all actions in their totality, find their culmination and completeness, in knowledge (of the Divine).

Accumulation of wealth, of more than what is actually required, causes anxiety and draws the individual away from the acquisition of intelligence. "It is easier for a camel to pass through the eye of a needle than a rich man to enter into

*heaven." A balance of wealth and knowledge leads to wisdom regarding what
is real and what is unreal.*

The supremacy of knowledge (4-34 to 4-39)

4-34   *tad viddhi pranipātena
                             pariprashnena sevayā
                             updeksyanti te jnānam
                             jnāninas tattvadarshinah*

Learn that by reverence (prostrating yourself), by questioning, and by
service. The seers and the wise ones will teach you that knowledge.

*"When the disciple is ready, the Guru will appear". Sat Guru or God in the
form of man knows the state of being of every aspirant. He leads the earnest
disciples gradually to where they can receive spiritual guidance. The earthly
Guru is he who has had experiences of God. Just as a lamp can light another
lamp, the Guru will transmit knowledge to the disciple who has prostrated
himself at his feet. Through devotion and enquiry at the feet of the teacher
regarding real and unreal, bondage and freedom, the disciple will gain insight
of spirituality. But dictatorship by the Guru is the sign of a Pseudo Guru.*

*In the end, the scriptures, the experiences of the mind, experiences during
meditation and the direct experiences and dreams must agree. Faith comes
first then knowledge, then experience of God. When God bestows His grace of
insight and wisdom, the disciple begins to understand reality. The disciple then
passes it to the masses, leading to the process of universal emancipation.*

4-36   *api ced asi pāpebhyah
                             sarvebhyah pāpakrittamah
                             sarvam jnānaplavenai 'va
                             vrijinam samtarishyasi*

If thou happen to be the worst of all sinners, still shalt thou be able to sail
across all the sins on the raft of knowledge.

*The enlightened perform action that would lead them to liberation. The same
action performed by the ignorant binds him further to the world.*

4-37
> *yathai 'dhāmsi samiddho 'gnir*
> *bhasmasāc kurute 'rjuna*
> *jnānāgnih sarvakarmāni*
> *bhasmasāt kurute tatha*

O Arjuna, as the blazing fire burns to ashes the firewood, so does knowledge burn all actions to ashes.

Sanchita Karma: - *Bears fruit in the distant future.*

Agamin Karma: - *Bears fruit in the near future.*

Prarabdha Karma: - *Being currently worked out.*

4-38
> *na hi jnānena sadrisam*
> *pavitram iha vidyate*
> *tat svayam yogasamsiddhah*
> *kālena 'tmani vindati*

Verily there is no purifier in this world like knowledge. He that is perfected in yoga realizes it in his own heart in due time.

A man wakes up after a horrible dream, breathes a sigh of relief and thanks God it was only a dream. In the same manner when one returns to the original blissful state through knowledge he sees the nothingness of this temporary world.

4-39
> *sraddhāvān labhate jnānam*
> *tatparah samyatendriyah*
> *jnānam labdhvā param shāntim*
> *acirenā 'dhigacchati*

He, who has reverence and faith, is steadfast and continent, gains wisdom and having gained wisdom, he very soon achieves the supreme peace.

The quest to know God requires maximum zeal and faith. Obedience to the preceptor, through whole-hearted service and in-depth inquires of God will facilitate progress in the acquisition of knowledge. God being the knower of past, present and future, and the redeemer, dictates when each being will receive this knowledge.

The fire of knowledge burns the first two and prarabdha is totally ignored and so rendered harmless.

4-41   *yogasamnyastakarmānam*
                        jnānasamchinnasamshayam
                        ātmavantam na karmāni
                        nibadhnanti dhananjaya

He who has dedicated all his actions to God, O Dhananjaya (Arjuna),
whose doubts have been cut asunder by wisdom and who is self-possessed,
cannot be bound by action.

*The divine plans trains and disciplines the individual souls gradually to
perfection. This process is the antidote to God's Maya or Illusion. Unlike the
mundane who gets trapped by creation, the Yogi gets anchored to the self. He
has no doubt about this and continues to serve humanity with his senses, mind
and intellect.*

4-42   *tasmād ajnānasambhutam*
                        hritstham jnānāsinā 'tmanah
                        chittvai 'nam samshyam yogam
                        ātistho 'ttistha bhārata

Hence O Bhārata (Arjuna), having cut asunder this doubt in your heart,
born of ignorance, by the sword of knowledge, betake yourself to yoga and
stand up to fight.

*Right knowledge produces right action. All evils originate because of doubt or
indecisiveness, which in turn is caused by ignorance of what is real.*

Action pertains to nature not atma (5-15 to 5-17)

5-15   *nā 'datte kasyacit pāpam*
                        na cai 'va sudritam vibhuh
                        ajnānenā 'vritam jnānam
                        tena muhyanti jantavah

The all-pervading soul does not share anybody's sin or virtue. Wisdom
is shrouded in ignorance; hence it is that created beings fall victims to
delusions.

*All of creation including man is the play of the all-pervading consciousness.
Creation is made up of matter, the five elements. Matter cannot affect*

consciousness or God. God in turn is not perturbed by the good and bad of individuals

5-16

**jñānena tu tad ajñānam
yeshām nāshitam ātmanah
teshām ādityavaj jñānam
prakāshayati tat param**

But in case of those whose ignorance has been overcome by wisdom, knowledge shines forth like the sun revealing the supreme self.

5-17

**tadbuddhayas tadātmānas
tannisthās tatparāyanāh
gacchanty apunarāvrittim
jñānanirdhutakalmashāh**

Meditating on Him, fully identified with Him, bearing steadfast loyalty to Him, turning to Him as the ultimate refuge, their sins are washed away by wisdom. Such men attain a state from where they do not have to return.

Discrimination, meditation and samadhi are the stages of God realization.

The four types of virtuous men (16-19)

7-16

**caturvidhā bhajante mām
janāh sukritino 'rjuna
ārto jijñāsur arthārthi
jñāni ca bharatarshabha**

O Best of Bharatas (Arjuna), the virtuous who worship me belong to four types - distressed ones, knowledge-seekers, wealth-seekers and wise ones.

When Draupadi was about to be de-robed in the presence of so many, she called on Sri Krishna and the Lord relieved of her distressed.

When Swami Vivekananda relentlessly sought knowledge, the Lord gave. The few who seek spiritual knowledge have received it.

Wealth comes easily to the religious-minded for the Lord provides without hesitation.

The jnani through the help of the Lord can perceive through intuition, that Brahman is the reality while the universe and the beings are all mere superimpositions on it. Adoring Brahman is his worship.

These four types of worshippers are virtuous because of their right understanding.

7-17   ***teshām jnāni nityayukta***
                ekabhaktir vishishyate
                priyo hi jnānino 'tyartham
                aham sa ca mama priyah

Among them, the wise one who is ever centred in the Divine, given to single-minded devotion, is the highest. For I am exceedingly dear to him and he to Me.

The Jnani is dearer to the Lord because he sees himself as one with God and creation.

7-18   ***udārāh sarva evai 'te***
                jnāni tv ātmai 'va me matam
                āsthitah sa hi yuktātmā
                mām evā 'nuttamām gatim

All of them are Noble indeed, but I regard the seer as my very self. For being God-centred, he seeks refuge in me and knows it to be the highest ideal.

7-19   ***bahunām janmanām ante***
                jnānavān mām prapadyate
                vāsudevah sarvam iti
                sa mahātmā sudurlabhah

The wise devotee, at the end of many cycles of birth, finds refuge in Me, realizing the truth that Vasudeva is all. Rarest of all is such a noble soul.

Vasudeva here means the all-pervading consciousness. It is easy to say that God is everything. However, only a few, through experience have gained conviction of this, They have become the true spiritual leaders of the society.

10-38   *dando damayatām asmi*
                 nitir asmi jigishatām
                 maunam cai 'vā smi guhyānām
                 jnānam jnānavatām aham

I am the sceptre of those who rule; I am statesmanship of those who seek victory; of secrets I am silence and among the wise, I am wisdom.

Sceptre – the staff of a monarch, the symbol of just punishment, not only for the convicted but also for society to see. Just as disease is the punishment for carelessness and misuse of the body, the sceptre is God's grace maintaining law and order.

Niti or statesmanship is the sound political policy that fosters mutual relationship and promotes divinity. The secret of the formula that makes the syrup of Coca Cola is necessary for the survival of Coca Cola Company. Similarly the secrets of God's knowledge is divulged to only those who are pure in heart and have a craving for it.

Nature or action is always bustling with sound, while God, the original and all pervading consciousness is always absolute silence. The knower of absolute silence realizes that it is most eloquent and readily accessible. When the spiritual aspirant and Brahman are in bonded relationship separation is not thought of. The two have become one. This wisdom, the Lord said is Himself.

12-12   *shreyo hi jnānam abhyāsāj*
                 jnānād dhyānam vishishyate
                 dhyānāt karmaphalatyāgas
                 tyāgācchāntir anantaram

Knowledge is indeed better than the yoga of practice; meditation is better than knowledge. Better than meditation is renunciation of the fruit of action. Such renunciation brings instant Peace.

Ritualistic practice is repeated or abhyasa. It is religion for the conventionals and purohits as it was inhereted and done mechanically. The reason is not known by them. There are others who know but do not practice yet there are others who know and meditates on Divinity in manifestations. The yogi is the best of man practices. A bird snatched a piece of meat from the butcher's shop. Immediately other birds followed him, fighting among them selves as they raced to snact it. To avoid the inevitable, the bird dropped the meat and then rested quietly on a branch. Giving and sharing is renunciation – the way to peace.

13-12   **adhyātma-jnānanityatvam**
                       tattvajnānārtha-darshanam
                       etaj jnānam iti proktam
                       ajnānam yadato 'nyathā

Constancy in the knowledge of the Spirit, insight into the end of the knowledge of Truth - this is declared to be (true) knowledge and all that is different from it is non-knowledge.

By removing what is ignorance that which remains is knowledge. Those who are ignorant tend to be vain and full of self-esteem. They seek to injure others, are revengeful, crooked, disrespectful, dirty, fickle, self-indulgent and long for objects that gratify the senses. Egoistic, their idea of happiness revolves around the body and its earthly attachments. They identify themselves with their children, spouse, home etc. Likes and dislikes make them restless. Enmeshed in frivolous social life they lack devotion and refuse to study the scriptures.

13-18   **jyotishām api taj jyotis**
                       tamasah param ucyate
                       jnānam jneyam jnānagamyam
                       hridi sarvasya vishthitam

He is the light of all lights and is said to be beyond darkness (ignorance). He is knowledge itself, object of knowledge and is attainable through knowledge. He dwells in all hearts.

The sun and moon glows and the earth bustles with life, but at the end of a day of Brahman (Kalpa) they cease to exist, because they are powered by the universal God. He who is meditating with his eyes closed in a dark room is aware of himself only because of the one illuminating soul. The perceptive senses, the thinking mind and the reasoning intellect gets their lumination from the cosmic Consciousness or the Atma. One must realize that ultimate truth exists inside. It is only then that he or she will see God in all of creation.

13-19   **iti kshetram tathā jnānam**
                       jneyam co 'ktam samāsatah
                       madbhakta etad vijnāya
                       madbhāvāyo 'papadyate

Thus I have told you in brief about the field (kshetra) and knowledge and the object of knowledge. Knowing this, My devotee becomes fit to attain union with Me.

Concentration is the essence of success in understanding and knowledge. Full attention to God makes one united with Him

13-35   **kshetrakshetrajnayor evam**
              antaram jnānacakshushā
              bhutaprakritimoksham ca
              ye vidur yānti te param

Those who thus perceive, with the eye of wisdom, the distinction between the Field and its Knower, and the liberation of beings from (the bondage of) prakriti (nature), attain the highest goal (the Supreme).

With the eyes closed and the mind and intellect gradually brought under control and made ineffective the aspirant is made aware of intuitive of the presence of God and His world. His sojourn in earthly life is now coming to an end.

15-10   **utkrāmantam sthitam vā 'pi**
              bhunjānam va gunānvitam
              vimudhā nā 'nupashyanti
              pashyanti jnānacakshusah

The ignorant do not see Him when He quits a form or dwells in it, possessed of gunas and enjoying these. But those who have eyes of wisdom see.

The acquisition of intuitive faculty is the only means to know that God resides in one's body. Lack of it causes one to be controlled by external objects, the mind and intellect. In this state, the individual can only experience, while travelling from body to body, birth after birth.

15-15   **sarvasya cāham hridi sannivishto**
              mattah smritir jnānam apohanam ca
              vedais ca sarvair aham eva vedyo
              vedāntakrid vedavid eva cāham

I dwell in everybody's heart; memory and knowledge proceed from Me and their loss as well. It is I Whom the Vedas seek to know. I am the author and knower of Vedānta.

A devotee of the Lord loses memory because the Lord decides what he should remember so that he can swiftly achieve realization. The academic is allowed to retain as much knowledge as he strives for as he is earthly bound.

16-23   **yah shāstravidhim utsrijya**
               vartate kāmkāratah
               na sa siddhim avāpnoti
               na sukham na parām gatim

He who casts aside the scriptural law and acts according to the promptings of his desire, does not attain perfection, happiness or the supreme goal.

Following the scriptures one gains happiness and prepares himself for the supreme goal, which is liberation.

16-24   **tasmāc chastram pramānam te**
               kāryākāryavyavasthitau
               jnātvā sāstravidhānoktam
               karma kartum ihā 'rhasi

Therefore, let the scriptures be your authority in deciding what ought to be done and what ought not to be done. Having known what is said in the ordinance of the scriptures you should act here.

The enlightened man has intrenalized the scriptures. What he thinks, speaks and does is in unison with the scriptures. The Cosmic Will has become his knowledge.

18-18   **jnānam jneyam parijnātā**
               trividhā karmacodanā
               karanam karma karte 'ti
               trividhah karmasamgrahah

Knowledge, knower and that which is known - these three motivate action. The instrument (senses), the object and the agent (doer) - these are the threefold basis of action.

Academic knowledge, object of knowledge as perceived by the senses, and the Jivatman the knower, comprises the triad of knowledge.

Action, the instrument and the objects make up the triad of karma or action.

Governed by the triad, the mind, the speech and the body perform respective functions.

18-19   **jnānam karma ca kartā ca**
               tridhai 'va gunabhedatah
               procyate gunasamkhyāne
               yathāvacchrinu tānyapi

Sānkhya philosophy affirms that knowledge, action and the doer (agent) are of three kinds only, according to the gunas, which predominates in each. Hear of them duly from Me.

Sankhya philosophy by sage Kapila is the authority on the three fold nature of man. Knowledge and action can be understood based on the competency of the students, namely - first rate, mediocre and backward.

18-20   **sarvabhuteshu yenaikam**
               bhāvam avyayamikshate
               avibhaktam vibhakteshu
               taj jnānam viddhi sāttvikam

Know that knowledge flowing from the sattva guna sees the single Imperishable One in all beings and the undivided among the divided.

Sattvika knowledge knows the imperishable to be one, although varieties come out of it. Nothing can be added to it or nothing can be subtracted. This is unity in diversity.

18-21   **prithaktvena tu yaj jnānam**
               nānābhāvān prithag vidhān
               vetti sarveshu bhuteshu
               taj jnānam viddhi rājasam

Know that knowledge to be of the nature of rajas, which sees diversity in diverse entities, each apart from the other.

The rajasika knowledge sees diversity. It sees Atman belonging to different species, castes, colours and nationalities. This castes deluded knowledge causes separatism and keeps the devotee in bondage.

18-22 **yat tu kritsnavad ekasmin**
kārye saktam ahaitukam
atattvārthavadalpamca
tat tāmasam udāhritam

That knowledge, which takes the part for the whole, ignores truth and reason and is trivial in concept, is said to be of the nature of tamas.

The belief of tamasika people is that the body only exists, it is made up of the five elements and that God is the images that are worshipped. They are ignorant of God as Consciousness. They cause disharmony at religious gatherings and places of worship as they think that they are the one and only champions and defenders of religion. Their understanding and reasoning goes counter to truth and so they aught to be treated as nuisances because of their whims and fancies.

18-70 **adhyeshyate ca ya imam**
dharmyam samvādamāvayoh
jnānayajnena tenāham
ishtah syāmiti me matih

And if any man studies this sacred discourse of ours, I shall consider that he worships Me through the yajna of knowledge.

Reading and practising Gita is one of the highest forms of worship of the Lord. The more we know of the workings of the God, the more we will adore and worship Him, and this is the purpose of life. His drama is vast and endless and it becomes the alternative to useless mundane thinking, speaking and practicing of day to day actions.

Mind and Meditation

1-30
na ca saknomy avasthātum
bhramati 'va ca me manah
nimittāni ca pasyāmi
viparitāni kesava

I am unable to stand; my mind whirls as it were; and Keshava, I see adverse omens.

Body and mind are interrelated; a change in one will cause a change in the other. At the sight of his kith and kin and teachers Arjuna saw bad omen and consequently his body and mind became weak. Attachment to family and teacher got in the way of duty.

2-44
bhogaisvarya prasaktānām
tayā 'pahrtacetasām
vyavasāyātmikā buddhih
samādhau na vidhiyate

There is no fixity of mind for them who cling to pleasure and power and whose discrimination is stolen away.

The desire-ridden people use their learning and speech to hunt after vulgar enjoyments. They use the ritualistic part of the Vedas to justify their desires. They are like the vultures that fly high on their learning but their enjoyments are in the carcasses of human desires, lust and greed. Mind and sense control are far from their thoughts.

2-67
indriyānām hi caratām
yan mano 'nuvidhiyate
tad asya harati prajnām
vāyur nāvam ivā 'mbhasi

Just as a strong wind tosses a ship on the wide ocean, the mind and intellect that yields to the roving senses carries away his discrimination.

As a rudderless ship cannot get to its destination so the mind that runs after the roving senses and sense objects gets lost in the mundane world, without any chance of self realization

3-6   *karmendriyāni samyamya*
                             ya āste manasā smaran
                             indriyārthān vimudhātmā
                             mithyācārah sa ucyate

The self-deluded fool who remains holding his organs in check, but all the
same dwells in his mind the objects of sense, is called a hypocrite.

*Sin and virtue accrue based on the state of the mind and not from bridling the
senses. If the Sadhaka sits in the meditative pose but the mind drifts without
sincere and conscious efforts to sublimate it, then this is hypocrisy.(story of two
friends)*

3-42   *indriyāni parāny āhur*
                             indriyebhyah param manah
                             manasas tu parā buddhir
                             yo buddheh paratas tu sah

The senses are said to be superior to the body. The mind is superior to
the senses. Superior to the mind is intellect: and what is superior to the
intellect is Atman.

*Freedom is determined by what governs our actions. When we act at the
prompting of our senses we are the least free than if we act according to our
mind. If we reason with our intellect we are even freer and if we surrender to
the Almighty Will or atman then freedom is at its maximum.*

6-5   *uddhared ātmanā 'tmānam*
                             na 'tmānam avasādayet
                             ātmai 'va hy ātmano bandhur
                             ātmai 'va ripur ātmanah

Let a man raise himself by his own self; let him not debase himself. For he
is himself his friend and himself his foe.

*No one but the individual can remove himself from his path of realisation.
Constant struggle in life is the aspirant's best friend. Continuous criticism from
the masses keeps him always alert.*

Favourable eviroment – (10, 11)

6-10   *yogi yunjita satatam*
                        ātmānam rahasi sthitah
                        ekāki yatacittātmā
                        nirāshir aparigrahah

The yogi should constantly try to concentrate his mind on the Supreme Self, dwelling in solitude, self-controlled, desireless and free from hankering for possessions.

The way of the mind is to be always active; first it should be made to focus on the glories of the Lord by way of repetition (japam) of sacred words (mantram). This can be achieved in solitude. Solitude is the process of one being in a place where no one else is aware of his presence and he also is not aware of the presence of others. To further aid meditation, the thought of possessions and extravagant bodily needs must be brought to bare minimum. Unbridled lust is the last obstacle a disciple must overcome and keep at bay, for continued progress in meditation. Dwelling on carnal thoughts is a sign of lack of self-control.

6-11   *shucau deshe pratisthāpya*
                        sthiram āsanam ātmanah
                        nā 'tyucchritam nā 'tinicam
                        cailājinakushottaram

He should firmly be seated on a clean spot, neither too high nor too low, covered with sacred grass (kusha), a deerskin and a cloth, one on top of the other.

In today's society, where the sacred grass or deer skin is not available the aspirant can sit in front of the home altar on a warm seat with the room temperature comfortable. The best time is early morning before others awake.

The method (12-15)

6-12   *tatrai 'kāgram manah kritvā*
                        yatacittendriyakriyah
                        upavisyā 'sane yunjyād
                        yogam ātmavishuddhaye

Then taking his place on the seat, with a steadfast mind, controlling thought and senses, he should practise yoga for purification of soul.

Mind is like a wretched dog. It has to be constantly trained or otherwise it gets lost in the sense objects. If it is made to think of God, then it will come under the control of the individual, thereby aiding in self-purification.

6-13
　　　　samam kāyashirogrivam
　　　　dhārayann acalam sthirah
　　　　samprekshya nāshikāgram svam
　　　　dishas cā 'navalokayan

Holding the head and neck in a straight line with the spine the yogis should be erect and still, looking fixedly at the tip of his nose, without allowing his eyes to wander.

If a snake were to crawl on the body of a person in meditation he will not be aware of its presence. If the spinal cord is positioned in a completely vertical position breathing and good thoughts are harmonized.

6-14
　　　　prashāntātmā vigatabhir
　　　　bhahmacārivrate sthitah
　　　　manah samyamya maccitto
　　　　yukta āsita matparah

Serene and fearless, firm in the vow of celibacy and dedicated in his service to the Guru, the Yogi must regularly practise meditation with his mind turned to Me and intent on Me alone.

With the body erect and sitting in padmasan position sloth and laziness are overcome. Most of all it helps in keeping one celibate. Observance of continuous celibacy, increases both mental and physical powers. It purifies the intellect and invigorates the intelligence. Intuitive knowledge is automatic; therefore unity with pure consciousness or God is the result. This is the elixir of life.

6-15
　　　　yunjann evam sadā 'tmānam
　　　　yogi niyatamānasah
　　　　shāntim nirvānaparamām
　　　　matsamsthām adhigacchati

Thus the yogi, subduing his mind, remaining steadfast, attains to supreme peace of Nirvana that is in Me.

A tourist will first secure his place of stay before he goes sight seeing. Seek first the knowledge of the self before you wander in the world care free, otherwise, at the time of death you will be in anxiety.

6-19
**yathā dipo nivātastho
ne 'ngate so 'pamā smrtā
yogino yatacittasya
yunjato yogam ātmanah**

'As the lamp in a windless place does not flicker' - this is the simile used for the disciplined mind of a yogi practicing concentration on the Self.

When the mind is completely sheltered against the wind of desire unbroken concentration is the result.

6-25
**sanaih-sanair uparamed
buddhyā dhrtigrhitayā
ātmasamstham manah krtvā
na kimcid api cintayet**

With his intellect set in firmness let him attain quietude little by little; with the mind fixed on the self let him not think of anything else.

Firmness is the outcome of a disciplined life. A learned person can be firm but when it comes to sensual pleasures his academic learning is of no use. Whereas the one anchored in the Self never sways.

6-26
**yato yato niscarati
manas cancalam asthiram
tatas-tato niyamyai 'tad
ātmany eva vasham nayet**

Whenever the restless fidgety mind runs berserk let the yogi apply restraint and bring it back under the sway of the self-alone.

Small harmful desires are to be fulfilled but the destructive ones are to be mercilessly eliminated by the sword of discrimination. Since mind always has to be in something, let it be on the Lord and His glories.

6-27
prasāntamanasam hy enam
yoginam sukham uttamam
upaiti sānta rajas am
brahma bhutam akalmasam

Supreme Bliss verily comes to that yogi whose mind is calm; whose passions are pacified, who has become one with Brahman and who is sinless.

6-34
cancalam hi manah krsna
pramāthi balavad drdham
tasyā 'ham nigraham manye
vāyor iva suduskaram

The mind verily is, O Krishna, restless, turbulent, strong and obstinate. I deem it as hard to control as the wind.

The word "Krishna" means "to plough and process". The mind is always shifting and when it does not get what it wants it is like the tiger is. The mind is like the leech. If you deny it of its wants it gets tougher and then becomes uncontrollable.

6-35
sri bhagavān uvāca
asamsayam mahābāho
mano durnigraham calam
abhyāsena tu kaunteya
vairāgyena ca grhyate

The Lord said:Doubtless, O mighty-armed, the mind is restless and hard to control; but practice and non-attachment, O son of Kunti can control it.

When one succumbs to the desires of the mind, bad habits become his nature and restlessness ensues. However, these habits can be removed through practice of sense control and replacing them with noble thoughts or thoughts of the glories of the Lord.

8-8
abhyāsa-yogayuktena
cetasā nā 'nyagāminā
paramam purusham divyam
yāti pārthā 'nucintayan

O Partha (Arjuna), by steadfast practice of yoga, with unwavering mind and thought concentrated on the Supreme Divine Being, one attains to Him.

Constant contemplation of deities of choice is called abhyasyoga. Eventually the spiritual aspirant loses body consciousness and merges with the Cosmic Self. It is like peeling off the skin from the fruit . God is called Purusha because He resides in the puri or the body.

12-6
        ye tu sarvāni karmāni
mayi samnyasya matparāh
ananyenai 'va yogena
mām dhyāyanta upāsate

12-7
        teshāmaham samuddhartā
mrityusamsārasāgarāt
bhavāmi nacirāt pārtha
mayyāveshitacetasām

But those, who surrender all their actions to Me taking Me to be the supreme, who turn to Me seated in their paths of yoga are saved by Me from drowning in this world, which is otherwise known as the ocean of death. (**Trans. 12-6 & 12-7**)

12-12
        shreyo hi jnānam abhyāsāj
jnānād dhyānam vishishyate
dhyānāt karmaphalatyāgas
tyāgācchāntir anantaram

Knowledge is indeed better than the yoga of practice and meditation is better than knowledge. Better than meditation is renunciation of the fruit of action. Such renunciation brings instant Peace.

Ritualistic practice is repeated or abhyasa. It is religion for the conventionals and purohits as it was inherited and done mechanically. The reason is not known by them. There are others who know but do not practice yet there are others who know and meditate on Divinity in manifestations. The yogi is the best of man practices. A bird snatched a piece of meat from the butcher shop, immediately other birds followed him, fighting among them selves as they raced to snatch it. To avoid the inevitable, the bird dropped the meat and then rested quietly on a branch. Giving and sharing is renunciation - the way to peace.

13-25   *dhyānenātmani pashyanti*
                          kecid ātmānam ātmanā
                          anye sāmkhyena yogena
                          karmayogena cā 'pare

Some realize the Self in the self by the self-resorting to meditation. Others betake themselves on the path of knowledge; still others by following the path of action.

18-52   **viviktasevi laghvāshi**
                          yatavākkāyamānasah
                          dhyānayogaparo nityam
                          vairāgyam samupāshritah

18-53   **ahamkāram balam darpam**
                          kāmam krodham parigraham
                          vimucya nirmamah sānto
                          brahmabhuyāya kalpate

Dwelling in solitude, eating but little, controlling speech, body and mind, and ever engaged in meditation and concentration and taking refuge in dispassion, the yogi sees the Self in himself as he turns away from desire, brutality and arrogance. Rising above attractions and repulsions he acquires realization in this very life. (**Exp. For 18-52 & 18-53**)

Man being a gregarious being, always looks for the company of others. Smooth relationships are the mark of civility. However, a yogi feels pestered by people and solitude becomes the diet for his introverted life. Contemplating on the Self is his relaxation.

Lightness of body and clarity of mind is advantageous on the spiritual path. Preservation of the vital fluid preserves and conserves vital energy, so intake of food is naturally reduced.

Speech is reduced, as the individual is not wanting to socialize; yet he attracts fellowship of the God-minded people. Every movement in his body is for a purpose and not out of habit and restlessness. He has arrived at serenity and calmness. Through experience and conviction he realizes that the Self is the end for him now and after. The Yogi is like a ripe fruit. He has severed connection with worldly affairs. (**Exp. For 18-52 & 18-53**)

Celibacy and Renunciation

3-4

> *na karmanām anārambhān*
> *naishkarmyam puruso 'shnute*
> *na ca samnyasanād eva*
> *siddhim samadhigacchati*

A man cannot achieve freedom from action by simply abstaining from work nor can he reach perfection by simply renouncing work.

Nature is the school for the Jivatman. Graduation here is when it transcends activities, or is at a state of perfection. At the end of a lifetime, the masses are like unripe fruits. They are not ready to stand-alone, as they are still attached to the world. Desireless action is actionless or sanyasa.

Selfless service is renunciation (5-1 to 5-14)

5-1

> *arjuna uvāca*
> *samnyāsam karmanām krishna*
> *punar yogam ca samsasi*
> *yac chreya etayor ekam*
> *tan me bruhi suniscitam*

Thou art talking, O Krishna, in the same breath of the renunciation of action and of its selfless performance. Tell me for certain which is the better of the two.

5-2

> *sri bhagavān uvāca*
> *samnyāsah karmayogas ca*
> *nihsreyasakarāv ubhau*
> *tayos tu karmasamnyāsāt*
> *karmayogo vishishyatte*

The Blessed Lord said:Both renunciation and action lead to deliverance. But of the two, the selfless performance of action is superior to its renunciation.

Aspirants who want to escape the turmoil of the worlds should willingly serve the world but should not be bound by it. Detached action allows the aspirants to experience the divine possibilities, thereby perfecting his union with God.

5-3   *jneyah sa nityasamnyāsi*
                       yo na dvesti na kānksati
                       nirdvandvo hi mahābāho
                       sukham bandhāt pramucyate

He who neither hankers nor loathes, O Mighty-armed, should be known
as one possessed ever of the spirit of renunciation. Such a man, set free
from conflicts, easily attains freedom from bondage.

*The karma yogi is the true sanyasa as he has mastered the art of doing selfless
duty. He has no dislike for any work that falls in his lot nor does he escape
doing work by pretending that he is poised in equilibrium.*

5-5   *yat sāmkhyaih prāpyate sthānam*
                       tad yogair api gamyate
                       ekam sāmkhyam ca yogam ca
                       yah pashyati sa pashyati

Both men of renunciation and of action reach the same status or goal. He
who looks with an equal eye on both action and renunciation is a true seer.

*Right knowledge will guide to right action and right action culminates in
knowledge.*

5-6   *samnyāsas tu mahābāho*
                       duhkham āptum ayogatah
                       yogayukto munir brahma
                       nacitrenā 'dhigacchati

Renunciation without (karma) yoga, O Mighty-armed, becomes the cause
sorrow only. The sage, betaking himself to karma-yoga soon attains to the
Absolute.

*A sanyasa is a philosopher as he translates yoga principles into practice. He
willingly and with goodness serves the society; then, like a ripe fruit he gradually
detaches himself from the mundane world and becomes anchored to the Self.*

5-7   *yogayukto visuddhātmā*
                       vijitātmā jitendriyah
                       sarvabhutāmabhutātmā
                       kurvann api na lipyate

He who is pursuant of selfless action, pure of soul, master of self, has subdued his senses, sees others as his own self, though he acts, is not bound by action.

5-8
nai 'va kimcit karomi 'ti
yukto manyeta tattvavit
pashyan srinvan sprisan jighrann
asnan gacchan svapan svasan

The man who is united with the Divine and knows the truth thinks, "I do nothing at all" while seeing, hearing, touching, smelling, tasting, walking, sleeping, breathing;

5-9
pralapan visrijan grihnann
unmishan nimishann api
indriyāni 'ndriyārtheshu
vartanta iti dhārayan

The seer who is tuned with God thinks, "I do nothing at all" for in seeing, hearing, touching, smelling, tasting, walking, sleeping, breathing, speaking, purging, grasping, opening or closing the eyes, he holds that only the senses are engaged with the sense-objects.

5-10
brahmany ādhāya karmāni
sangam tyaktvā karoti yah
lipyate na sa pāpena
padmapattram ivā 'mbhasā

He who acts, having forsaken attachment, consigning his actions to God, is not tainted by sin even as a lotus leaf is not wetted by water.

The Lotus leaf growth and sustenance totally depends on water, in the same way man's birth and sustenance is dependent on karma.

5-11
kāyena manasā buddhyā
kevalair indriyair api
yaginah karma kurvanti
sangam tyaktvā 'tmashuddhaye

The yogins (men who follow the path of action) perform action with only body, mind and understanding or with only the senses, forsaking attachment and egoism, for purifying their souls.

5-12
> *yukta karmaphalam tyaktvā*
> *shantim āpnoti naisthikim*
> *ayuktah kāmakārena*
> *phale sakto nibadhyate*

The man, tuned with the Divine, attains to abiding peace-forsaking desire for the fruits of action; the man not similarly tuned becomes attached to the fruits through desire and comes under bondage.

5-13
> *sarvakarmāni manasā*
> *samnyasyā 'ste sukham vashi*
> *navadvāre pure dehi*
> *nai 'va kurvan na kārayan*

The self-controlled person having mentally renounced action dwells happily in the city of nine gates neither doing any thing, nor setting others to do anything.

Various types of actions-

    Nitya: *- Obligatory - e.g. eating, sleeping etc.*

    Naimitya: *- Observation of holy days - Shivratri celebration etc.*

    Kamya: *- Earthly achievements*

    Nishiddha: *- Prohibitive acts - unethical actions*

The Yogi engages himself only in nitya karmas, as the others are ego-driven. The nine gates are two ears, two eyes, two nostrils, mouth, and excretory and reproductive organs. The Atman is the monarch of this city, with the ego, mind, intellect, life-energy and the senses as His ministers. For the Yogi the Self has no role to play and he is aware of this but for the earth bound person, the consciousness of self is not present but only the organs are in action.

5-14
> *na kartritvam na karmāni*
> *lokasya srijati prabhuh*
> *na karmaphalasamyogam*
> *svabhāvas tu pravartate*

The lord of the self does not either ordain the doer ship or the doings of beings. There is no nexus between action and its fruits. It is Nature that performs action.

5-26
kāmakrodhaviyuktānām
yatinām yatacetasām
abhito brahmanirvānam
vartate viditātmanām

The sages, freed from lust and anger, of disciplined mind, having self-knowledge attain supreme liberation and are surrounded on all sides by the blessed state of existence in Brahman.

Nyasa – *sublimation*

Sanyasa – *total sublimation*

The world is to the sanyasi as the shadow is to the individual.

6-1
sri bhagavān uvāca
anāsritah karmaphalam
kāryam karma karoti yah
sa samnyāsi ca yogi ca
na niragnir na cā 'kriyah

The Blessed Lord said:He who performs his duty without an eye to the fruits of action is a samnyāsi (a true renouncer) and a yogi (a true worker) too. Not so is he who has abjured the sacred fire or activity in all forms.

A sanyasin is a karma yogi and lives a life of celibacy. The Lord corrects Arjuna's misconception that a Sanyasi is free from active duties. The Sanyasin must engage in duty for duty-sake so that he sets an example for society to follow and at the same time he does not look for any reward. It is the same with the karma yogi.

6-2
yam samnvāsam iti prāhur
yagam tam viddhi pāndava
na hy asamnyastasamkalpo
yogi bhavati kascana

O Pandava, make sure that what they call samnyasa is another name for yoga; for none can be a yogi who has not given up his selfish peroccupations.

Sankalpa - is to create a formative imagination in the mind about the fruits of action. These promises or preoccupations become desires. A Yogi or sanyasa is one who is free from Sankalpa.

6-3   ***ārurukshor muner yogam***
                      karma kāranam ucyate
                      yogārudhashya tasyai 'va
                      shamah kāranam ucyate

Action is said to be the means resorted to by the sage who wishes to attain to yoga. Once he attains the yoga, serenity is said to be the means he resorts to.

Swami Pranavananda of Bharat Sevashram Sangha does not recommend a secluded mountain cave to grow into spiritual life, instead he recommends a life that is laden with karma yoga. This he said would lead into perfect meditation, as karma yoga is the best sacrifice and purifier. The daily practice of meditation brings clarity of mind and eventually leads to serenity. Serenity leads to equilibrium, which in turn leads to perfection in thoughts, words and deeds and also into becoming a Yogi.

6-4   ***yadā hi ne 'ndriyārtheshu***
                      na karmasv anushajjate
                      sarvasamkalpasamnyāsi
                      yogārudhas tado 'cyate

When one has renounced all desires and is no longer enamoured of the objects of sense or of action, he is said to have attained yoga.

Sankalpa is to determine upon a goal — the desired fruit. To be a sanyasin or yogi, all sankalpas must be abandoned. Furthermore the external world, which is a projection of the mind, has no more of existence to him, as the senses are withdrawn. In the last stage or Samadhi, obligatory bodily duties are suspended and the yogi is at rest like a calm, serene ocean.

6-6   ***bandhur ātmā 'tmanas tasya***
                      yenā 'tmai 'vā 'tmanā jitah
                      anātmanas tu shatrutve
                      vartetā 'tmai 'va shatruvat

To him who has conquered his self by self, his self proves a friend, but the self of the uncontrolled proves hostile like a foe.

Replacing the base nature with divine qualities, gradually and then fending off the resurgence of evil ones is the task of the aspirant. Man's enemy is his own mind. He is the master of his destiny.

6-14   ***prashāntātmā vigatabhir***
                        bhahmacārivrate sthitah
                        manah samyamya maccitto
                        yukta āsita matparah

Serene and fearless, firm in the vow of celibacy, subdued in mind, let him sit, poised in the state of harmony, his mind turned to Me and intent on Me alone.

With the body erect and sitting in a padmasan position, slothful and lazy feelings go away. Most of all it helps in maintaining celibacy. Observance of continuous celibacy, increases both mental and physical powers. It purifies the intellect and invigorates the intelligence. Intuitive knowledge is automatic; therefore unity with pure consciousness or God is the result - it is the elixir of life.

6-17   ***yuktāhāravihārasya***
                        yuktacestasya karmashu
                        yuktasvapnāvabodhasya
                        yoga bhavati duhkhahā

Know that he whose yoga makes him temperate in his intake and movements, in japa and reading of the scriptures in his sleep and waking hours shall have all his worldly sorrows negated.

Just by putting the mind to a serene, calm state, the body is also made relaxed or least trouble free. Moderation in exercise, eating, sleeping etc. makes the body movements like that of the calm planets. A sound mind and healthy body is necessary for meditation.

6-46   ***tapasvibhyo 'dhiko yogi***
                        jnānibhyo 'pi mato 'dhikah
                        karmibhyas cā 'dhiko yogi
                        tasmād yogi bhavā 'rjuna

The yogi is deemed superior to ascetics, superior to men of knowledge even; he is also superior to ritualists. Therefore be you a yogi, O Arjuna.

Ascetic – one who undergoes self- induced mortification so that they can enjoy here and here after.

Rituals – one who follows the teachings of the scriptures of how to appease the gods. Their goal in life is limited to their faith in these rituals. The individual with knowledge of the scriptures is intelligent. He may even leave his sannyas life and the austerity of a yogi but he uses his knowledge for his self-glorification instead of glorification of God, his fame will eventually dwindle.

8-11
yadaksharam vedavido vadanti
vishanti yad yatayo vitarāgāh
yad icchanto brahmacaryam caranti
tat te padam samgrahena pravakshye

I shall tell thee briefly that state (and how to attain it) which those versed in the Vedas call the Imperishable, which ascetics free from attachment attain to, and desiring which the sādhakas practise continence.

Through celibacy the physical energy of man gets converted into spiritual energy. This spiritual energy together with continued discipline develops the faculty of medha or intuitiveness.

13-8
indriyārthesu vairāgyam
anahamkāra eva ca
janma mrtyu jarā vyādhi
duhkha dosānudarsanam

Man grows in devotion to the Lord in direct proportion to his detachment from the objects of the senses.

13-10
asaktir anabhisvangah
putra dāra grhādisu
nityam ca samacittatvam
istānistopapattisu

The mind is in a state of equilibrium, unattached and indifferent to the welfare or otherwise of children, spouse and home.

Life is a series of experiences that are temporary. Relationship is part of this temporary experience. This ownership must be overcome by discrimination and by contemplation. Death severs all relationships and everything is seen as possessions of the creator. Loss of loved ones no longer causes pain as even mindedness in all eventuality makes the seeker poised in harmony.

13-11
> **mayi cā 'nanyayogena**
> **bhaktir avyabhicārini**
> **vivikta desa sevitvam**
> **aratir janasamsadi**

The aspirant will reside in a clean place, fear from tigers, thieves and snakes, his mind pinpointed and focused on Me.

God is real and the mundane world is unreal. The conviction of this makes one a sanyasa renouncer. The aspirant retires to an ashram conducive to meditation and seeks the company of holy ones or makes his or her mind always attached to the God.

home in an ashram. At the ashram, after a while, he lives in seclusion.

13-12
> **adhyātma-jnānanityatvam**
> **tattvajnānārtha-darshanam**
> **etaj jnānam iti proktam**
> **ajnānam yadato 'nyathā**

Spiritual knowledge will lead to self-knowledge. All other knowledge is misleading.

By removing what is ignorance that which remains is knowledge. Those who are ignorant tend to be vain and full of self-esteem. They seek to injure others, are revengeful, crooked, disrespectful, dirty, fickle, self-indulgent and long for objects that gratify the senses. Egoistic, their idea of happiness revolves around the Body and its earthly attachments. They identify themselves with their children, spouse, home etc. Likes and dislikes make them restless. Enmeshed in frivolous social life they lack devotion and refuse to study the scriptures.

13-13
> **Tjneyam yat tat pravakshyāmi**
> **yaj jnātva 'mritam ashnute**
> **anādi matparam brahma**
> **na sat tannā 'sad ucyate**

The path towards self-realisation involves the following – humility, freedom from arrogance, reluctance to destroy life, forgiveness, simplicity, service to Guru, external cleanliness, determination about the path to liberation, control over natural tendencies, aversion towards sensual pleasures and absence of egoism. No longer is the aspirant affected by the repetitive cycle of birth and death, by wealth and possessions, by spouse, children and domestic bonds. The heart of the yogin remains poised in an attitude of equilibrium towards good and bad, knowing that God alone is real. The yogin in search of the self remains firm in his faith, becomes a recluse, shuns mundane company and resolute in search for knowledge of the real. The opposite of these are egoism, arrogance and ignorance. They are the cause of all worldly movements.**(meaning for 13-8 to 13-12)**

God is manifested and unmanifested. The three gunas cause variations in the manifested state but when these three gunas are in equilibrium the manifested state ceased to exist. Nirgun Brahman or pure conciousness is ever constant, there is no beginning and no end as there is neither manifestation or unmanifestation. Great souls can realize this state through meditation. The need for enquiry into knowledge and ignorance (Purusha and Prakriti) ends.

18-2   **kāyānām karmanām nyāsam**
                sannyāsam kavayo viduh
                sarvakarmaphalatyāgam
                prāhus tyāgam vicakshanāh

The Blessed Lord said:The wise understand by renunciation the complete giving up of actions motivated by desire and the discerning define relinquishment as giving up the fruit of all actions.

Sanyasa is the renouncing of the desires that hankers for good health, wealth, long life, progeny, name and fame, title and status. These are called kamya karma, as they are sown seeds that causes rebirth or hindrances to liberation. Tyaga or relinquishment is the abandonment of the fruit of actions (obligatory, occasional and optional works. e.g. duties of a housewife decreases as she advances in her pregnancy and stops after delivery as she is left to tend to her baby)

18-4   **nishcayam shrinu me tatra**
                tyāge bharatasattama
                tyāgo hi purushavyāghra
                trividhah samprakirtitah

O Best of Bharatas (Arjuna), hear now from Me. My own conclusion about tyāga (relinquishment). O Lion among Men (Arjuna), it is declared to be of three kinds, depending on one's nature, inclinations or propensities.

The three types of works that should be given up are: -
  i)   Yajna or sacrifices
  ii) Giving or donating
  iii) Austerities

The whole process of renunciation is gradual. After the lower desires are fulfilled and the unrealistic ones are renounced by way of acceptance through knowledge, then the individual moves steadily to higher thinking or closer to self realization. Nature is the best teacher of renunciation.

Examples: *- the ripe fruit separates from the tree, the new born baby detaches from the mother, the rays are separated from the Sun and a student after graduation leaves the school. Likewise, the individual soul through experience and knowledge should fulfill its worldly sojourn and gradually become one with the all-pervading Soul. One is called a Yogi because he has speedened up this process while the ordinary man lingers on aimlessly in his journey of life.*

18-5   *yajnadānatapahkarma*
                    na tyājyam kāryam eva tat
                    yajno dānam tapas cai'va
                    pāvanāni manishinām

Acts of sacrifice, gifts and austerity should not be abandoned, but performed. Sacrifice, gifts and austerity purify the wise.

After his self-education by fulfilling his kamya karma (worldly desires), the aspirant comes to realize the limitations of the world. It is now time to break the cocoon of earthly life and fly freely in the bliss of divine life. His duties are restricted to teaching the world through sacrifice, donating and giving and through austerity or control of the senses.

18-6   *etānyapi tu karmāni*
                    sangam tyaktvā phalāni ca
                    kartvyaāni 'ti me pārtha
                    nishcitam matamuttamam

O Partha, but even these acts must be performed without attachment or regard for their fruits. This is My considered and best view.

The mind that gives expands; the mind of the wise gets purified through sacrifice, gifts and austerity. Giving to these holy ones has a purifying effect to the giver. This is the sure way to make the world a better place for all.

Reliquishment of sattvika nature (18-9 to18-12)

18-9   ***kāryam ity eva yat karma***
                     niyatam kriyate 'rjuna
                     sangam tyaktvā phalam cai'va
                     sa tyāgah sāttviko matah

O Arjuna, a prescribed action that is done as a duty, giving up attachment and desire for its fruits, is regarded as sattvic form of relinquishment.

18-10   ***na dvesty akushalam karma***
                     kushale nā 'nushajjate
                     tyāgi sattvasamāvishto
                     medhāvi chinnasamshayah

The wise one, endowed with sattvika traits, free from doubts, given to renunciation, is not averse to disagreeable action nor is he attached to agreeable action.

Non-action is the characteristics of the atman. As the clean mirror reflects the things and events so the Atma witnesses and records all actions but is not affected by them. The disciple or Sthitaprajna who is anchored in the knowledge of atman never sways from the truth.

There are those who see work as a burden and at very opportune moment seeks the easy way out. Success for them is to get the maximum gain and sensual measure with minimum effort. They disguise themselves as religious individuals. On the other hand the stalwarts are always looking for opportunities to contribute to the welfare of society unconcerned of the agreeable or disagreeable nature of the task at hand. Their understanding is simple, pure and clear.

18-11   *na hi dehabhritā shakyam*
                  tyaktum karmānyasheshatah
                  yas tu karmaphalatyāgi
                  sa tyāgi 'tyabhidhiyate

No human being can refrain from action altogether. But he who abandons
the fruits of action is said to be the relinquisher.

*The human body is an embodiment of ceaseless actions; some are involuntary
like breathing, while other functions are voluntary. Life can be compared to
an aeroplane journey. When it is in the air, it moves over mountains, valleys,
boisterous ocean and seas. Sometimes it encounters turbulent winds, which
cause fear to the passengers, but quickly the captain and crew give assurances
that everything is under control. The passengers realize that they are in able
hands and so place their minds on higher thoughts. Man likewise must continue
the journey of his life discharging his duty in the midst of ups and downs,
keeping always his mind that at the end of the journey is liberation.*

18-12   ***anishtam ishtam mishram ca***
                  trividham karmanah phalam
                  bhavaty atyāgmām pretya
                  na tu sannyāsinām kvacit

After death threefold is the fruit of action for those who are attached – good,
evil and mixed. But for those who have chosen the path of renunciation
there will be no fruit to reap at all.

*The cycle of birth and death is a continuation based on the life one lives. Rebirth
is dictated by and inherent in the type of characteristics of the previous lives.
Beings of evil actions are first hurled into hell and then are reborn as beasts.
Men of good actions enjoy heavens and then reborn as heavenly bodies. While
men of good and bad actions enjoy heaven and hell and then they are reborn in
favorable environments, the noble ones that master the transmigration of birth
and death (the perfect) exist as bodies are already established in the Self.*

18-49   ***asaktabuddhih sarvatra***
                  jitātmā vigatasprihah
                  naishkarmasiddhim paramām
                  sannyāsenā 'dhigacchati

He who is fully non-attached, self-controlled and devoid of desire, attains supreme perfection of naishkarmya through renunciation of the fruits of action.

A karma yogi or a sanyasin is constantly involved in activities. He does not have a permanent place of rest. Any place is his residence. As myriad forms of work comes to him so they are as being dispersed in the same manner water flows under a bridge. Ill feelings, good feelings, likes and dislikes, don't arise in his mind as he has reached the state of placidity due to his mastery of his original identity, his soul. Desires have been conquered through wisdom.

CHAPTER - III

Signs of a person in relationship with God

Stable and even-minded

2-54
arjuna uvāca
sthitaprajnasya kā bhāsha
samādhisthasya keshava
sthitadhih kim prabhāsheta
kim āsita vrajeta kim

Arjuna said:O Kesava (Krishna), what then are the signs of the man who, passing through the stage of samādhi (tranquil contemplation), has been able to become steadfast in wisdom? How does he speak? How does he sit? How does he walk about?

The path to liberation and liberation itself is one and the same. As one moves step by step, he experiences temporary bliss, which becomes total bliss when he goes into samadhi.

2-55
sri bhagavān uvāca
prajahāti yadā kāmān
sarvān pārtha manogatān
ātmany eva ātmanā tushtah
sthitaprajnas tado 'cyate

O Pārtha, when a man surrenders all his innate desire to and his spirit remains content in hisself, he deserves to be described as stable-minded.

Kama – when the mind goes outside, grabbing for happiness. The Brahma jnani is he who has tuned his attention inwardly and found total bliss. Kama no longer exists in him.

2-56   *duhkhesv anudvignamanāh*
                       sukheshu vigatasprihah
                       vitarāgabhoyakrodhah
                       sthitadhir munir ucate

The man who remains unflurried in the midst of sorrow, indifferent to happiness, who has mastered passions, fear and anger, may be called stable-minded.

Fondness is the attachment to someone. The individual is unable to see defects in the other. Fear is the thinking that one can get hurt or killed. One who has fear cannot succeed in this world, or in the world beyond. Anger is the state of unbalanced mind caused by dislikes.

2-57   *yah sarvatrā'n abhisnehas*
                       tat-tat prāpya shubhāshubham
                       nā bhinandati na dveshti
                       tasya prajnā pratishthitā

Stable-minded is he who has no fondness for anything, who is not elated or provoked to disgust if good luck or bad overtakes him.

A Jnani neither praises nor utters words of censure. Figuratively he is looking down in the world with an equal eye.

2-58   *yadā samharate cā 'yam*
                       kurmo 'ngāni 'va sarvashah
                       indriyāni 'ndriyāthebhyas
                       tasya prajnā partishthitā

Him we call stable-minded who withdraws his senses from sense-objects much in the same way as the tortoise withdraws into its own shell.

Pratyahara – the act of withdrawing the senses and then resting peacefully in the Self. Like a snake charmer, the jnani has mastered the treacherous and undependable senses.

2-59

vishayā vinivartante
nirāhārasya dehinah
rasavarjam raso 'py asya
param drishtvā nivartate

Sense-objects cease to have their appeal for the man who desists from enjoying them with his senses. But the hankering goes on lingering. This too vanishes when the stable-minded man has his vision of the Supreme.

*An aspirant is he who by constant reasoning sees the nothingness in sense objects while **the jnani** is he who has overcome this by reasoning and is resting peacefully in the Self. **The ordinary man** just craves for sense pleasures incessantly.*

2-60

yatato hy api kaunteya
purushasya vipascitah
indriāni pramāthini
haranti prasabham manah

O Son of Kunti, the unruly passions gain control over the mind of even a well-disciplined and discerining man.

The aspirant constantly fights with his wayward senses. In the beginning he loses. However, through determination the scale tilts and he wins in the end, but he must always be on the guard otherwise, they are always ready to cause havoc.

2-61

tāni sarvāni samyamya
yukta āsita matparah
vashe hi yasye 'ndriyāni
tasya prajnā pratisthitā

He who worships me with single-minded devotion, can control his senses and rest with his mind centred in me. In fact, he who has thus controlled his senses is called the stable-minded sage.

To suppress the senses is not the way of spiritual success because the mind sooner or later will rebound with even greater force. Instead the mind should be made to occupy itself on the glories of God. Mind cannot be on two conflicting tasks simultaneously.

2-62   *dhyāyato visayān pumsah*
                      sangasteshu 'pajāyate
                      sangāt samjāyate kāmah
                      kāmat krodho 'bhijāyate

2-63   *krodhād bhavati sammohah*
                      sammohāt smritivibhramah
                      smritibhramsād buddhināsho
                      bundhināshāt pranashyati

Thoughts centered on objects of the senses gives birth to attachments. From attachments springs desires; frustrated desire transforms itself into anger. Anger causes forgetfulness of what is right and what is wrong.Thus, together with the death of the conscience brings fogetfullness of all the instructions of the scripties and the teachers.With the loss of this memory a man is no longer able to discriminate between the good the bad, between what is abiding and what is temporary. And when this power of discernment is lost man ceases to be man in the true sense. (2-62 and 2-63)

Good thoughts make a man good and evil ones destroys him. (Story of the Harlot and the Holy Man). Anger is the temporary unstableness of the mind and lunacy is the permanency of this violent unstableness. (Story of man going to work and got destructed by female.) (exp2-62 and 2-63)

2-64   *rāgadveshavimuktais tu*
                      vishayān indriyaish caran
                      ātmavashyair vidheyātmā
                      prasādam adhigacchati

But the self-controlled man, free from likes and dislikes, who moves about among sense-objects with his senses subdued, attains peace of mind.

The sense objects and the senses are all slaves of the yogi because the mind is made to dwell in the purity of the atma. In the ordinary man pleasures of the senses and sense objects becomes the driving force. If the senses are used for worship and surrender to God then they can become useful instruments. (Give chart of surrender during Aarti)

2-65
prasāde sarvadukhānām
hānir asyo 'pajāyate
prasannacetaso hy āsu
buddhih paryavatisthate

With the calmness of mind thus attained, all sorrows of man are set at rest, for the mind of such a tranquil person is soon concentrated.

Evil seen outside is a projection of the mind. Yudhisthira was sent out to find a bad man but found none. Likewise Duryodhana could not find a good man in the whole world. All of creation is divinity in different settings

2-66
nā 'sti buddhir ayuktasya
na cā 'yuktasya bhāvānā
na cā 'bhāvayatah shāntir
ashāntasya kutah sukham

The undisciplined man is lacking in reason, nor can such a man have meditation. Without meditation, he cannot have peace. And how can one be happy without peace?

Right understanding comes from right action or self-culture. Bhavana is the state of mind of right understanding. This is the process for peace and spirituality

2-67
indriyānām hi caratām
yan mano 'nuvidhiyate
tad asya harati prajnām
vāyur nāvam ivā 'mbhasi

When the mind goes chasing one of the senses, that particular sense runs away with the man's intelligence very much as the wind drives the barge on the water.

As a rudderless ship cannot get to its destination, likewise a mind that runs after the roving senses and sense objects gets lost in the mundane world, with no chance of self realization

2-68
tasmād yasya mahābāho
nigrihitāni sarvashah
indriyāni 'ndriyārthebhyas
tasya prajnā pratisthitā

O Thou of Strong Arms, one whose senses have in all ways been withdrawn from their objects, has attained the state of serene wisdom.

The senses cannot be made to stand still. However, the attitude with which they are used differs.

The eyes being the most dangerous should be trained to see the opposite sex as temples of God. Eating to maintain a fit body is virtue but to satisfy the tongue at every calling is sin. When all the senses become the slave of the individual then God will reveal Himself.

2-69
yā nishā sarvabhutānām
tasyām jāgarti samyami
yasyām jāgrati bhutāni
sā nishā pashyato muneh

That which is night to all beings, is to the disciplined man day; that which is day to all beings, is night to the Self-cognizing Muni.

On the physical plane the tigers sees well in the night vice-versa to man. One in a specific profession e.g. a thief sees opportunities for stealing while others are oblivious to them. The mundane man sees the world as the end all of his life and makes all preparations for his success in it. However, the spiritual man does not get involved with the permanency of the mundane but focusses and rests peacefully in the Self. He sees God in all earthly relationships

2-70
āpuryamānam achalapratistham
samudram āpah pravishanti yadvat
tadvat kāmā yam pravishanti sarve
sa shantim āpnoti na kāmakāmi

The ocean remains full in its fullness even after the rain water drains into it. It does not surge forward to cross the limits of the shoreline but remains undisturbed in its totality. In the same way the cries and hankerings of the ignorant enter the seer and blends into him. It affects him not. It disturbs not his abiding peace. But peace eludes the man running after fleeting desires.

The minds of the realized souls are filled to capacity just like the ocean which never changes although the rivers of the world empty into it. He realizes his temporary stay in the body and as such does not get modified by the variations of the incoming pairs of the opposites. The enlightened ones have moved beyond the physical and mental planes. They have become examples for society and a role model for the aspirant.

2-71
> ***vihāya kāmān yah sarvān***
> ***pumāms carati nihsprihah***
> ***nirmamo nirahamkārah***
> ***sa shāntim adhigacchati***

The man who renounces all desires and goes about shaking himself free from attachment, egotism and hankering for pleasures, attains peace.

The feeling of agency that is created by "I and mind" creates bondage. All the vast waters span of the world seems separate but in reality they are one body. The ego in this manner through ignorance sees individuality in beings. Spiritual life destroys this egoism of "I and mine-ness". By not desiring for mundane thing, eventually the feeling of the all-pervading conscious prevails.

2-72
> ***eshā brāhmi-sthitih pārtha***
> ***nai 'nām prāpya vimuhyati***
> ***sthivā 'syām antakāle 'pi***
> ***brahmanirvānam ricchati***

O Pārtha, this is Brāhma-sthiti (resting in Brahma, the divine state, life eternal). Having once attained this, one becomes free from confusion. Remaining steadfast in that state at the last hour, one attains to divine bliss.

Brahma nirvana or aparaksha – anubhuti is the state above the working of the mind and intellect. Jivanmukti is the stage lower, meaning that the individual still holds on to the body. The Jivatmans are a rung below the latter stage. As the aspirant progresses on the path of purification of the mind his work changes automatically by the Lord's grace. It can be compared to the two stages of difference – before and after birth. If through continuous practice, at the time of death one can maintain this state of nirvana he will attain liberation.

3-26   *na buddhi bhedam janayed*
                        ajnānām karma sanginām
                        jojayet sarva karmāni
                        vidvān yuktah samācaran

Let not the wise man unsettle the mind of ignorant people attached to karma. By their persistant activity let the wise induce the others to work and action.

To work for results is far better than being lazy or idle. For a mundane man, to say he is at peace by being quiet and inactive is hypocrisy. The enlightened should not disturb this type of person with talks about "do duty for the duty's sake" he will never understand

Attainment of bliss

5-18   *vidyāvinayasampanne*
                        brāhmane gavi hastini
                        shuni cai 'va svapāke ca
                        panditāh samadarsinah

Sages look with an equal eye on all whether a gentle and scholarly Brahmin, an outcaste, a cow, an elephant or even a dog.

Nescience creates plurality while omniscience reveals unity in multiplicity.

5-19   *ihai 'va tair jitah sargo*
                        yeshām sāmye sthitam manah
                        nidosham hi samam brahma
                        tasmād brahmani te sthitāh

Even here on the mortal plane (existence) is conquered by those whose mind rests steadfast in equality. Brahman is free from taint and is the same in all beings. Hence these persons rest secure in Brahman.

5-20   *na prahrishyet priyam prāpya*
                        no 'dvijet prāpya cā 'priyam
                        sthirabuddhir asammudho
                        brahmavid brahmani sthitah

Such a man who has realized Brahman is well-poised, free from delusions and rests secure in Brahman. Hence he is neither elated with getting what is agreeable, nor upset by what is disagreeable.

An aspirant who is established in pure consciousness does not think of likes and dislikes. His schooling in mundane life is over. He is free from lust and grief. Light and bliss shines in him.

5-21
> *bāhyasparsheshv asaktātmā*
> *vindaty ātmani yat sukham*
> *sa brahmayogayuktātmā*
> *sukham aksayam ashute*

He who is indifferent to outside sound and glamour enjoys undiluted bliss. He becomes one with Brahman and the inheritor of this bliss which has no end.

When the sadhaka reaches the state of God consciousness, the bliss he so patiently and deliberately sought he gets by the Grace of God; he now discards all thoughts of falling back to worldly pleasures.

5-24
> *yo 'ntahsukho 'ntarārāmas*
> *tathā 'ntarajyotir eva yah*
> *sa yogi brahmanirvānam*
> *brahmabhuto 'dhigacchati*

The yogi who finds his happiness within, his delight within and his lights, too, within, becomes divine himself and achieves supreme liberation (oneness with the Brahman).

Just when one gets accustomed to pleasures from relationships and sense objects, it usually ends in sorrow and distress.

5-25
> *labhante brahmanirvānam*
> *rishayah kshinakalmashāh*
> *chinnadvaidhā yatātmānah*
> *sarvabhutahite ratāh*

The seers whose sins have been cleansed, whose doubts have been revered, whose minds are well-poised, who delight in doing good to all beings, attain to supreme liberation (oneness with the Brahman).

A Rishi is one who is completely detached from the world.

5-26   ***Kāma krodha viyuktānām***
                   yatinām yatacetasām
                   abhito brahmanirvānam
                   vartate viditātmanām

The sages, freed from lust and anger, of disciplined mind, having self-knowledge, attain supreme liberation (are surrounded on all sides by the blessed state of extinction in Brahman).

Nyasa *– sublimation*
Sanyasa *– total sublimation*

The world is to the sanyasas as a shadow is to a person.

Perfection in yoga

6-8   ***jnānavijnāna triptātmā***
                kutastho vijitendriyah
                yukta ity ucyate yogi
                samalostāshmakāncanah

That yogi is steadfast who is satisfied with knowledge and wisdom, who remains unshaken, who has conquered the senses, to whom a clod, a stone and a piece of gold are the same.

The enlightened soul has gone beyond the desires for the accumulation of worldly riches as he sees them as temporary possessions. He has discovered the bliss of his origin and shows he is travelling without the baggage of gold and other precious items and modifications of creation.

6-21   ***sukham ātyantikam yat tad***
               buddhigrāhyam atindriyam
               vetti yatra na cai 'vā 'yam
               sthitas calati tattvatah

When he feels that supreme bliss which is perceived by the intelligence and which transcends the senses, and when established in it he never moves from the Reality;

6-22
yam labdhvā cā 'param lābham
manyate nā 'dhikam tatah
yasmin sthito na duhkhena
gurunā 'pi vicālyate

And having gained it, he thinks that there is no greater gain than that;
wherein established he is not shaken even by the heaviest affliction;

The Pandavas trials and tribulations were never looked up as sufferings for they
were deeply rooted in the thought that their bodies will go one day. They gave
up kingdom in search of eternal peace after the Mahabharata war.

6-29
sarvabhutastham ātmānam
sarvabhutāni cā 'tmani
ikshate yogayuktātmā
sarvatra samadarshanah

He who is united by yoga with the Divine, looks upon all beings with the
eyes of equality, seeing the Self in all beings and all beings in the Self.

The jivatmans are actually one cosmic entity that exist in all being as
consciousness. When the body, mind and intellect factor are sublimated then
this oneness is realized.

6-30
yo mām pashyati sarvatra
sarvam ca mayi pashyati
tasyā 'ham na pranashyāmi
sa ca me na pranashyati

He sees Me everywhere and sees all things in Me. I am never out of his
sight nor is he ever out of My sight.

The multitudes of being and the universe are the external sport of the Lord.

6-31
sarvabhutasthitam yo mām
bhajaty ekatvam āsthitah
sarvathā vartamāno 'pi
sa yogi mayi vartate

He who, firmly planted in unity, worships Me as dwelling in all beings,
that yogi lives in Me whatever be his mode of life.

The senses are mere instruments in the hands of understanding. They either get attached to the objects or repulsed. These pairs of opposites govern the behavior of mundane man but for the Godward bound, the senses are pushed aside as they see everything as temporary.

6-32   **ātmaupamyena sarvatra**
                      samam pashyati yo 'rjuna
                      sukham vā yadi vā duhkham
                      sa yogi paramo matah

O Arjuna, he who looks upon all with an equal eye, whether in joy or sorrow, as it they were in his own self, is considered to be a yogi par excellence.

In the same manner the limb of ones body does not hurt another limb. The yogi sees all beings as limbs of that one cosmic personality. There is the story of the holy man nursing a brother monk who had been beaten and thrashed. When the latter was asked if he could identify who was his assailant he replied " the hand that beat me some time ago is the same hand that is now nursing".

Divine traits of a disciple of devotion (sloka 12-13 to 12-20 in section "devotion and surrender" see p.)

Transcended Base Nature

14-22

sri bhagavān uvāca
prakāsham ca pravrittim ca
moham eva ca pāndava
na dvesti sampravrittāni
na nivrittāni kānkshati

The Blessed Lord said:O Pandava, the three gunas lead to manifestations, tendencies and delusions. He who is not inimical to them and yet does not wish to suppress them either, rises above the gunas.

The liberated souls are unaffected by the happenings of the world. They have transcended the three forces of nature. They no longer crave for or are disturbed by the loss of sleep as their bodies are reduced to bare minimum (tamas). Going regularly to mandirs, performing ritualistic worship etc. are done if it is their duty but they do not feel any loss if these actions are not done. (Rajas). Scriptural learning, listening to devotional songs and holy discourses, deep meditation are practiced by the holy ones, but if these doings (sattvika) are interrupted, there is no feeling of loss as the Brahma jnani is ever resting in Brahman.

14-23

udāsinavad āsino
gunair yo na vicālyate
gunā vartanta ityevam
yo 'vatishthati ne 'ngate

He who is unconcerned and undisturbed by the gunas and is well aware that the gunas alone operate never loses his composure (such a man is said to have transcended the gunas).

14-24

samaduhkhasukhah svasthah
samaloshtāshma kāncanah
tulyapriyāpriyo dhiras
tulyanindātmasamstutih

He who is alike in pleasure and pain, who is self-possessed, to whom clod of earth, stone and gold are all of equal value, who remains constant in the midst of things both pleasant and unpleasant, who regards praise and blame as same and is firm in determination is said to have transcended the gunas.

The active nature or gunas have assumed the form of man and other beings. These beings interact with each other thereby causing the likes and dislikes and the other pairs of opposites but the one who is fully rested in a super soul is not disturbed.

14-25
mānāpamānayos tulyas
tulyo mitrāripakshayoh
sarvārambhaparityāgi
gunātitah sa ucyate

He who is indifferent to either praise or insult, who is neither avengeful towards enemies nor indulgent towards friends, who has given up all activities that bear fruit covert or overt, doing only those necessary to maintain the body is said to be beyond the gunas.

Here the urge for the activity is selfless activity.

14-26
mām ca yo 'vyabhicārena
bhaktiyogena sevate
sa gunān samatityai 'tān
brahmabhuyāya kalpate

He who worships Me with unfaltering love transcends these gunas and becomes fit to attain oneness with Brahman.

The devotee worships God with form and through the grace of the Lord realizes Him to be also without form. When devotion and knowledge gets harmonized, liberation ensues.

Other Divine Qualities

2-15
yam hi na vyathayanty
ete purusam purusarsabha
sama duhkha sukham dhiram
so 'mrta tvāya kalpate

That man, O the best of men, is fitted for immortality, whom these do not torment, who is balanced in pain and pleasure and is steadfast.

Cessation of misery corresponds to the removal of ignorance. Earthly life is the school to acquire the knowledge that grief is a feeling that is related to body identification, whereas, realization of the Self eventually leads one to immortality

2-46
yāvān artha udapāne
sarvatah samplutodake
tāvān sarvesu vedesu
brāhmanasya vijānatah

To an enlightened Brahman all the Vedas are as useful as a tank when there is a flood everywhere.

The scriptures provide happiness on earth and in heaven but the realized soul basking in eternal bliss cares not for the temporary earthly joys.

2-52
yadā te moha kalilam
buddhir vyatitarisyati
tadā gantāsi nirvedam
srotavyasya srutasya ca

When your understanding transcends the taint of delusion, then shall you gain indifference to things heard and those yet to be heard.

Mankind is like a child looking for hidden coloured eggs during Easter. The Lord gradually allows new discoveries of the intricacies of his creation. The enlightened one who has made relationship with the Creator has no fascination for His creation, the Universe.

4-22
yadricchālābhasamtushto
dvandvātito vimatsarah
samah siddhāv asiddhau ca
kritvā 'pi ne nibadhyate

He who remains content with whatever falls to his lot, is free from envy, has soared beyond all pairs of opposites (like joy and grief), remains steadfast alike in success and failure, and though performing action, is not subject to bondage.

God provides for those who surrender to Him. The Lord in turn, provides for the needs of disciples, which is food and a few pieces of clothing. The disciple is happy to see the prosperity of all and never is he envious. He works with the philosophy that (feed and clothe the hungry then tell him about God).

7-3
manusyānām sahasresu
kascid yatati siddhaye
yatatām api siddhānām
kascin mām vetti tattvatah

Among thousands of men scarcely one strives for perfection, and of those who strive and succeed, scarcely one knows Me in truth.

All are entitled to liberation, some will get it in this very birth, some in a few births and some after countless births. Everyone in their own way knowingly or unknowinly are striving for it through, fullfilment, accomplishment, complete attainment, success, solving of a problem, maturity, final emancipation etc.

The path to perfection has many pitfalls but the rare aspirants that possess the fourfold virtues -
> *right attitude*
> *right understanding*
> *right adjustment*
> *right application*

Shall gain divinity.

10-4
buddhir jnānam asammohah
ksamā satyam damah samah
sukham duhkham bhavo 'bhāvo
bhayam cā 'bhayam eva ca

Intellect, wisdom, non-delusion, patience, truth, self-restraint, calmness, pleasure, pain, birth, death, fear and fearlessness.

Intellect – *the faculty of grasping matters subtle.*

Non delusion – *the clarity of the mind even in trying and critical situations.*

Patience – *kindly attitude of the mind even towards opponents and enemies.*

Truth – *accurate presentation of what has been seen, known and experienced.*

Calmness – *the practice of quietude of the mind and intellect.*

Self – restraint – *the control of the external senses of touch, taste, sight, smell and hearing*

10-5 **ahimsā samatā tushtis
tapo dānam yasho 'yashah
bhavanti bhāvā bhutānām
matta eva prithagvidhāh**

Non-violence, equal-mindedness, contentment, austerity, charity fame and ill-fame (are) the different states of existence. All proceed from Me alone.

Equanimity - *the lack of likes or dislikes during or after desirable or undesirable happenings.*

Austerity - *elimination of bad habits through rigorous self-discipline.*

Charity - *the giving of good and useful things to the deserving.*

By the grace of God, all these powers have been bestowed to the disciple.

16-1 **sri bhagavān uvāca
abhayam sattvasamsuddhir
jnānayogavyavasthitih
dānam damash ca yajnash ca
svādhyāyas tapa ārjavam**

Fearlessness, purity of mind, wise apportionment of knowledge and concentration, charity, self-control and sacrifice, study of the scriptures, austerity and uprightness are divine qualities.

Fear is the cause with the identification of body; fear that it can get hurt or that it can be killed. A person suffering from fear cannot elevate himself in life, and he is fit for nothing. Hindu Gods and Goddesses are symbols of fearlessness as they hold weapons in their hands. As an aspirant gets closer to God, fear is removed automatically.

Purity - *is when there is no distinction between the welfare of others and one's own self.*

Knowledge - *is the realization and one-pointed-ness that God alone is real and everything else is unreal. Union with God is His only goal.*

Sacrifice - *is the science of giving that which will be beneficial to the masses and at the same time, removing all traces of selfishness from the giver.*

Almsgiving - *to deserving people with genuine love, kindness and humility increases the coffers of the giver by manifolds.*

Scriptures - *the recordings of our saints and sages of their experiences during their time of deep contemplation.*

These texts rid man of superstitions and take him God-ward.

Austerity - *is the act of recasting ones mind, against his mode of life so as to make him spiritual.*

16-2   ***ahimsā satyam akrodhas***
                tyāgah sāntir apaisunam
                dayā bhutesv aloluptvam
                mārdavam hrir acāpalam

Non-injury, truth, absence of anger, renunciation, serenity, absence of calumny, compassion to beings, uncovetousness, gentleness, modesty, absence of fickleness.

16-3   ***tejah kshamā dhritih saucam***
                adroho nā'timānitā
                bhavanti sampadam daivim
                abhijātasya bhārata

Vigour, forgiveness, fortitude, purity, absence of hatred, absence of pride, these belong to one born for a divine state, O Bharata.

Shi Bhagawan said - Oh Arjuna those who are desirous of acquiring the pure sattvic stage are born with the following twenty qualities-fearlessness, truthfulness, in speech and action, devotedness towards yoga and a propensity to give alms in proportion to capabilities. They are able to control the senses, perform the five yajnas, recite the scriptures and observe austerities. By nature they are simple, envious of none, truthful, free from anger, ever ready to sacrifice, peace abiding, non critical of others, merciful, free from greed, temperate, ashamed to entertain unholy thoughts or deeds, not frivolous, brave and upright, ever forgiving, clear in physical habits, not hostile or belligerent and not egoistic. (**Exp. for 16-1,16-2 and 16-3**)

CHAPTER - IV

Qualities of a person not in relationship with God – Sinner

Origin of sin

3-37
> *sri bhagavān uvāca*
> *kāma esha krodha esha*
> *rajogunasamudbhavah*
> *mahāshano mahāpāpmā*
> *viddhy enam iha vairinam*

The Blessed Lord said:This is desire, this is wrath. It springs from the elements of rajas, is insatiable and ravenous. Know this to be an enemy in this world.

3-38
> *dhumenā 'vriyate vahnir*
> *yathā 'darso malena ca*
> *yatho 'lbenā 'vrto garbhas*
> *tathā tene 'dam āvrtam*

As fire is enveloped by smoke, as a mirror by dust, as an embryo by the womb, so is this covered by that.

The soul is veiled by desires. Desires are like smoke that cover fire. With a little discrimination, these desires are blown aside and the soul is revealed. The Rajasic veil is in the form of excessive effort to acquire worldly possessions while the Tamasic veil is like the embryo in a womb. Evolution out of this veil takes time.

3-39
āvritam jnānam etena
jnānino nityavairinā
kāmarupena kaunteya
duspurenā 'nalena ca

Knowledge is enveloped, O Son of Kunti (Arjuna) by this insatiable fire of desire, the eternal foe of the wise.

Desires can never be satisfied by the enjoyment of the objects of desires. Desires grow more and more, just as fire blazes when fuel is thrown into it. Although the wise tries to keep it at bay it always finds a way to reappear.

3-40
indriyāni mano budhir
asyā 'dhisthānam ucyate
etair vimohayaty esha
jnānam āvritya dehinam

It is said that it has its seat in senses, mind and intellect. Enveloping our wisdom through these, it casts its spell on the embodied soul.

When desires take control, the disciple is dragged by the base habits of lust and greed. The soul is the only thing to know. Desires are impossible to eliminate. In other words, if an alternative is not created then mundane life is the force of attraction and repulsion.

3-41
tasmāt tvam indriyāny ādau
niyamya bharatarshabha
pāpmānam prajahi hy enam
jnānavijnāna-nāshanam

Hence, O Greatest of Bharatas, first restraining the senses, slay this sinful desire, which seeks to destroy wisdom and power of discrimination.

Anything that obstructs spiritual growth is maya or illusion. The right understanding of the scriptures is knowledge and intuition of God as consciousness, is realization.

3-42
indriyāni parāny āhur
indriyebhyah param manah
manasas tu parā buddhir
yo buddheh paratas tu sah

The senses are said to be superior (to the body). The mind is superior to the senses. Superior to the mind is intellect. What, however, is superior to the intellect is He (the Atman).

Freedom is determined by what governs our actions. When we act at the prompting of the senses we are the least free. If we reason with our intellect we are even freer and if we surrender to the Almighty Will then freedom is at its maximum.

3-43   **evam buddheh param buddhvā**
                       samstabhyā 'tmānam ātmanā
                       jahi satrum mahābāho
                       kāmarupam durāsadam

Thus knowing the Atma as superior to the intellect, restraining the self by the self, slay, the enemy in the form of desire, Arjuna.

When maya or illusion is understood it disappears. Happiness associated with the body, senses and intellect is temporary. When atma is realized they become slaves to it.

Demonic qualities

16-4
     dambho darpo 'bhimānas ca
     krodhah pārusyam
     ajnānam cā 'bhijātasya
     pārtha sampadam āsurim

Ostentation, arrogance, and self-conceit, anger, harshness and ignorance belong to one born of demonic qualities.

Ostentation – *putting up a show of good behaviour and donning oneself in pompous permanents.*

Arrogance – *presuming that oneself is superior to the others.*

Conceit – *priding oneself on being educated, moneyed and high-born.*

16-7
     pravrittim ca nivrittim ca
     janā na vidur āsurāh
     na shaucam nā'pi cā'cāro
     na satyam teshu vidyate

Men of demoniac nature do not know what they ought to do and what they should refrain from doing. There is no truth in them or purity. There is not right.

Even animals refrain instinctively from wrong action but the demonic person's physical habits and doings are unclean. His utterances are misleading and false.

16-8
     asatyam apratishtham te
     jagadāhur anishvaram
     aparasparasambhutam
     kimanyat kāmahaitukam

They say that the world is void of truth or moral principles and is Godless and that it is created by the physical union of men and women. It is a product of lust and nothing else.

The infidels (disbelievers) the profligates, the atheist and the nihilists deny and defy the law of the land and also moral and ethical laws. They think that the world is perpetuated by lust and so make lust the better part of their life. They condemn religious institutions, ridicule the holy ones and holy orders and prevent others from taking to the path of religious life.

16-9
        etām drishtim avashtabhya
        nashtātmāno'lpabuddhayah
        prabhavanty ugrakarmānah
        kshayāya jagato'hitāh

Holding this view, these lost souls of mean understanding, are given to cruel deeds and are ill disposed. They are born for the destruction of the world.

16-10
        kāmam āshritya dushpuram
        dambhamānamadānvitāh
        mohād grihitvā 'sadgrāhān
        pravartante 'shucivratāh

Given to insatiable desire, full of bluster, pride and arrogance, clinging to wrong ideas through delusion, they work with unholy resolve.

16-11
        cintām aparimeyām ca
        pralayāntām upāshritāh
        kāmopabhogaparamā
        etāvad iti nishcitāh

Obsessed with innumerable cares, which would end only with (their) death, looking upon the gratification of desires as their highest aim they are assured that this is all.

They are like the camel although they experience pain from their sinful actions they continue to indulge in them. Driven by lust they amass a big family that they cannot support. They cry when their daughters get married yet they beget more. Money is wasefully spent on litigation but they don't try for correction through peace.

16-12
        āshāpāshashatair baddhāh
        kāmakrodhaparāyanāh
        ihante kāmabhogārtham
        anyāyenā'rthasamcayān

Bound by hundreds of ties of desire, given over to lust and danger, they strive to amass hoards of wealth, by unjust means, for the gratification of their desires.

16-13
idam adya mayā labdham
imam prāpsye manoratham
idam asti'damapi me
bhavishyati punar dhanam

This today has been gained by me; this desire I shall attain, this is mine and this wealth also shall be mine (in future).

16-14
asau mayā hatah shatrur
hanishye cā 'parān api
ishvaro'ham aham bhogi
siddho'ham balavān sukhi

This foe is slain by me. Others also I shall slay. I am the lord, I am the enjoyer, I am successful, mighty and happy.

16-15
ādhyo 'bhijanavānasmi
ko'nyo'sti sadrisho mayā
yakshye dāshyāmi modishye
ityajnānavimohitāh

"I am rich and well-born. Who is there like unto me? I shall sacrifice, I shall give, I shall rejoice," thus they (say), deluded by ignorance.

16-16
anekacittavibhrāntā
mohajālasamāvritāh
prasaktāh kāmabhogeshu
patanti narake'shucau

Bewildered by many thoughts, entangled in the meshes of delusion and addicted to the gratification of desires, they fall into a foul hell.

16-17
ātmasambhāvitāh stabdhā
dhanamānamadānvitāh
yajante nāmayajnais te
dambhenā 'vidhipurvakam

Self-conceited, obstinate, filled with the pride and arrogance of wealth, they perform sacrifices, which are so only in name with ostentation and without regard to rules.

Sacrifice has been taken over by ritualistic worship. Temples are built for advertisement and costly worship is worship void of devotion; instead they are done for name and fame.

16-18

> *ahamkāram balam darpam*
> *kāmam krodham ca samshritāh*
> *mām ātmaparadeheshu*
> *pradvishanto 'bhyasuyakāh*

They find fault with the true seekers and therefore fail to follow their footsteps. Pride and a vicarious pleasure to torture others, drives them to lust and anger. These malicious people hate Me Who dwells in their bodies and the bodies of others of others.

The little religious learning they have, they use to humiliate the holy ones by claiming that they are the authorities. Instead of using their bodies as temples of the Lord they defile it with lustful acts and also hurt others bodies, the abode. Their demise is inevitable.

17-5

> *ashāstravihitam ghoram*
> *tapyante ye tapo janāh*
> *dambhāhamkārasamyuktāh*
> *kāmarāgabalānvitah*

Those men, vain and conceited and impelled by the force of lust and passion, perform violent austerities, which are not ordained by the scriptures.

17-6

> *karshayantah sharirastham*
> *bhutagrāmam acetasah*
> *mām cai'vā'ntahsharirastham*
> *tān viddhy āsuranishcayān*

Being foolish they oppress the group of elements in their body and Me also dwelling in the body. Know these to be demoniac in their resolutions.

Torturing the body is an act not sanctioned by the scriptures. After practicing extreme torture to His body Gautama Buddha condemned all painful austerities

as unworthy and unprofitable. Lying on spikes, gazing at the sun, standing on
one leg with arm stretched may cause hallucinations but this not be thought of
as spirituality.(Explanation of both Sloka 5 and Sloka 6)

17-19   *mudhagrāhenā'tmano yat*
                          pidayā kriyate tapah
                          parasyo'tsādanārtham vā
                          tat tāmasam udāhritam

Austerity is said to be tāmasic in nature when it is practised through a
deluded understanding, by means of self-torture or for causing hurt to
others.

The intellects of people of tamasika nature are not fully developed, so their
ability to understand ideals is imperfect. Their understanding of austerity is to
torture the senses by exposing the body to extreme heat and cold and starvation,
not knowing what the result will be. Occasionally they may get some psychic
power, which they use to torment fellow humans.

Other sinful qualities
1-35   *nihatya dhārtarāstrān nah*
                          kā pritih syāj janārdana
                          pāpam eva 'srayed asmān
                          hatvai 'tān ātatāyinah

Oh Janardan! By slaying Duryodhana and other sons of Dhritarashtra
what pleasure will I get? By killing them we wil acrue sin.

Although the Kauravas were desperados (no criminal offences were new to
them), Arjuna out of sentimental weakness found it difficult to engage in war
with them.

1-37   *yady apy ete na pashyanti*
                          lobhopahatacetasah
                          kulaksayakritam dosham
                          mitradrohe ca pātakam

Although overpowered by the lust for power they cannot see the sins
arising out of the destruction of family and friends, should we, being aware
of the harm being done to our kith and kin not try to restrain ourselves
from this wrong doing? (**Trans. 1-36 &1-38**)

1-44

ahobata mahat pāpam
kartum vyavasitā vayam
yad rājyasukhalobhena
hantum svajanam udyatāh

Alas, we are bent on committing the grievous sin of slaying our kith and kin lured by the prospects of enjoying the pleasures of a kingdom.

2-33

atha cet tvam imam dharmyam
samgrāmam na karishyasi
tatah svadharmam kirtim ca
hitvā pāpam avāpasyasi

But if thou desist from fighting this righteous war, thou wilt be tainted with the sin of forsaking both duty and glory.

When an action is done knowing that it will delay or prevent one from realizing the self is an act of sin.

2-38

sukhaduhkhe same kritvā
lābhālābhau jayājayau
tato yuddhāya yujyasva
nai 'vam pāpam avāpsyasi

Hence treating alike weal and woe, gain and loss, victory and defeat, be ready for battle. Fighting in this way, thou shalt not incur sin.

3-12

ishtān bhogān hi vo devā
dāsyante yajnabhāvitāh
tair dattān apradāyai 'bhyo
yo bhunkte stena eva sah

The Gods, nourished by these sacrifices, will offer thee the pleasures thou seek. One who enjoys their gifts without making a return is verily a thief.

The world provides facilities because of the sacrifice of few people. The mother sacrifices for her child, education, clothing, food etc. These are sacrifices on her part. Since we take the sacrifices of others we too have to contribute, otherwise we become thieves.

3-13   *yajnashishtāsinah santo*
                          mucyante sarvakilbishaih
                          bhunjate te tv agham pāpā
                          ye pacanty ātamakāranāt

The good people, who feed upon the leftovers of the sacrifice, are absolved
from all sins. But the unrighteous who cook only for themselves feed on
sins.

*Any work is neither good nor bad but the motive makes it good or bad. If there
is no selfish or egotist motive it is but purely for the welfare of the masses, it is
good. King Yudhisthira of the Mahabharata once invited hundreds of people
from all walks of society with the intention of feeding and giving them gifts
but his motive was not intense and sincere enough as demonstrated by* **the
mongoose**. *It was done to a certain extent for pomp and glory.*

*There are five types of sacrifices – pancha yajna they form obligatory duties of
man.*
> *Deva Yajna - worship of Gods*
> *Rishi Yajna - worship of enlightened souls - books*
> *Pitri Yajna - worship of living parents and departed   ancestors*
> *Nara Yajna - worship for devoted service to mankind*
> *Bhuta Yajna- worship for relating and caring for all living beings*

*God has entered each nook an corner of His creation as the soul. The five
elements comprise the lower self. Performing these Yajnas or sacrifices is a
constant reminder that God is ever present.*

3-32   *ye tv etad abhyasuyanto*
                          nā 'nutisthanti me matam
                          sarvajnāna vimudhāms tān
                          viddhi nashtān acetasah

But those who enviously do not follow my teaching, know these witless
men, devoid of all wisdom know them to be lost.

*Moral and spiritual laws are no different from the laws of nature. Therefore,
the one who does not see the illusion of nature gets entangled or incurs sin.*

4-36   *api ced asi pāpebhyah*
                          sarvebhyah pāpakrittamah
                          sarvam jnānaplavenai 'va

vrijinam samtarishyasi

If thou happen to be the worst of all sinners, still shalt thou be able to sail across all sins on the raft of knowledge.

Knowledge that is the very inherent nature of man is ever active. His true self, frees him from sin.

5-10

**brahmany ādhāya karmāni
sangam tyaktvā karoti yah
lipyate na sa pāpena
padmapattram ivā 'mbhasā**

He who acts, having forsaken attachment, consigning his actions to God, is not tainted by sin even as a lotus leaf is not wetted by water.

The growth and sustenance of the Lotus leaf totally depends on water. In the same way man's birth and sustenance is dependent on karma.

5-15

**nā 'datte kasyacit pāpām
na cai 'va sukritam vibhuh
ajnānenā 'vritam jnānam
tena muhyanti jantavah**

The all-pervading soul does not share in any-body's sin or virtue. Wisdom is shrouded in ignorance; hence it is that created beings fall victims to delusions.

All of creation, including man is the play of the all-pervading Consciousness. Creation is made up of matter, the five elements. Matter cannot affect consciousness or God. God in turn is not perturbed by the good and bad of individuals.

CHAPTER - V

Death, after death and rebirth

1-36

*nihatya dhārtarāstrān nah
kā pritih syāj janārdana
pāpam evā 'srayed asmān
hatvai 'tān ātatāyinah*

What pleasure can be ours, O Krishna, after we have slain the sons of Dhritarastra? Only sin will accrue to us if we kill these malignants.

Although the Kauravas were desperados (no criminal offences were new to them), Arjuna out of sentimental weakness found it difficult to engage in war with them.

1-41

*samkaro narakāytai 'va
kulaghnānām kulasya ca
patanti pitaro hy esam
luptapindodakakriyah*

As a result of hybridisation, both the family, and the destroyers of the family are consigned to hell. The manes of their families also suffer degradation being deprived of their offerings of water and lumps of rice.

Prayers offered in the name of the departed while they are awaiting rebirth have a positive effect.

1-43

utsannakuladharmānām
manushyānām janārdana
narake niyatam vāso
bhavati 'ty anushushruma

O Janardana (Krishna), we have heard that those whose family traditions have gone to rack and ruin dwell eternally in hell.

2-11

sri bhagavāna uvāca
ashocyān anvashocas tvam
prajnāvadāms ca bhāshase
gatāsun agatāsums ca
nā 'nushocanti panditāh

The Blessed Lord said :Thou grievest for those who do not deserve to be grieved over, yet thou speaketh like a wise man. The wise grieve for neither the living nor the dead.

A pundit is one who knows the plan and purpose of the universe. He knows that death and rebirth are parts of this great plan just as it is usual for the Sun to set and rise. At the commencement of the Mahabharata, Arjuna forgot the great plan and so spoke as a wise man in the midst of his shivering. The Lord's purpose was to bring him out of this lapse of courage. Dronacharya and Bhishma understood the plan of the universe. They were ready to do battle, although because of principle, they were fighting on the opposite side of the Lord. Bhishma eventually told Arjuna how he could be slain. This was a display of fearlessness. The Lord asked Arjuna to harmonize his thoughts, words and deeds as he was thinking one way, speaking in another and acting yet in another. His personality was splitting. Sri Krishna was trying to prevent this.

2-13

dehino 'smin yathā dehe
kaumāram yauvanam jarā
tathā dehāntaraprāptir
dhiras tatra na muhyati

Just as the human body passes through the different phases of childhood,youth and decrepit old age, so it is with the soul taking on another body. The sage does not feel bewildered at this.

Staying unperturbed in good or bad situations is preparation to remain unperturbed at the time of death. The same conscious life force that is in the body stays unchanged in youth and in old age. Likewise it's the same after death and when it enters a new body at rebirth with the same inherent tendencies.

2-22   ***vāsāmsi jirnāni yathā vihāya***
                         navāni grihnāti naro 'parāni
                         tathā sharirāni vihāya jirnāny
                         anyāni samyāti navāni dehi

Just as a man puts off old worn-out clothes to put on new ones, so does the soul put away the worn-out body to take on a new one.

The mental makeup of a person never dies. As the individual souls sheds its cage of flesh and bone, the innate qualities enter his subtle body. At the appropriate time of rebirth, the promptings of the subtle mind dictate the form the new body will take. Just as the snake sheds its skin and is not disturbed by it, so man has to be calm at the time of giving up his body at the time of death.

2-27   ***jātasya hi dhruva mrityur***
                         dhruvam janma mritasya ca
                         tasmād aparihārye 'rthe
                         na tvam shocitum arhasi

One who is born is sure to die and one who dies is sure to be born. So thou shouldst not grieve over the inevitable order of things.

Committing suicide is not accepted simply because it is an interruption of the plan of Nature. Death by war or deliberate murder does not exclude the offender from sin. Natural death is spoken of here.

2-32   ***yadricchayā co 'papannam***
                         svargadvāram apāvritam
                         sukhinah ksatriyāh pārtha
                         labhante yuddham idrisham

O Partha (Arjuna), this war has, as it were, offered itself as an opportunity. It is like the gate of Heaven thrown wide open. Only the fortunate among the Kshatriyas get the chance of fighting such a war.

The Grace of God comes to everyone at the opportune moment. At this moment, with a little effort, great results can be achieved. However, many cannot recognize it or they walk away from it. As in the case of Arjuna and the

Pandava Brothers, who underwent endless trials and tribulations; fighting the war was an opportunity to them. Afterwards, they ascended to heaven.

2-34   **akirtim cā 'pi bhutāni**
                           kathayisyanti te vyayām
                           sambhāvitasya cā 'kirtih
                           maranād atiricyate

People will ever recount your infamy. To the honoured, infamy is surely worse than death.

The aim of the mundane man is to preserve life but for the hero preservation of the ideal even at the cost of his life is his goal. Losing honor and fame is his true death.

2-37   **hato vā prāpsyasi svargam**
                           jitvā vā bhokshyase mahim
                           tasmād uttishtha kaunteya
                           yuddhāya kritaniscayah

If thou art slain in battle, thou wilt attain heaven. If thou winnest victory, thou wilt enjoy all the pleasures that the earth has to offer. Hence, O Son of Kunti (Arjuna), set thy mind on war and rise.

A righteous war is needed to strike a balance between the good and the unrighteous. The bad must be slain and the good given the right to rule for even if they die, liberation is theirs.

4-5   **sri bhagavān uvāca**
                           bahuni me vyatitani
                           janmāni tava cā 'rjuna
                           tāny aham veda sarvāni
                           na tvam vettha paramtapa

The Blessed Lord said:O Arjuna, both thou and I have passed through many a life. I know all of them, thou dost not, O Chastiser of thy Foe (Arjuna).

Here the difference between an Incarnation and the Jivatman comes into play. An Incarnation is the manifestation of the cosmic consciousness whereas the Jivatma is a soul that is smeared by karma on the path to Cosmic Consciousness.

Krishna Bhagawan being sat-chid-ananda knows the past, present and future. Arjuna is dealing with his senses and reacting to circumstances around him.

4-9
janma karma ca me divyam
evam yo vetti tattvatah
tyaktvā deham punarjanma
nai 'ti mām eti so 'rjuna

He who understands my divine birth and activities in their true nature, O Arjuna, is no longer subject to re-birth but comes to Me.

The holy man who catches the true spirit of the Lord and His drama, transgresses the illusion of creation. They become lesser and lesser affected by worldly affairs while in the cage of flesh and bones. In this life they gradually merge with Pure Consciousness, thereby having no need to return to this world after death. The Gods and Goddesses that we worship were once Jivatmans but now are perfected souls. It is for this reason we worship holy men and women as we see God-like qualities in them. Only a few understand the incarnations and they pass this knowledge to the masses.

Falling from yoga (6-41 to 6-45)

6-41
prāpya punyakritām lokān
ushitvā shāshvatih samāh
shucinām shrimatām gehe
yogabhrasto 'bhijāyate

He who hath lapsed from yoga passeth to the world of the righteous and liveth there for many years. He is then born again into a rich and pious family.

Falling from yoga the devotee enjoys pleasure in the celestial heaven. His rebirth puts him in a home that is fit for his continued evolution.

6-42
athavā yoginām eva
kule bhavati dhimatām
etad dhi durlabhataram
loke janma yad idrisham

Or he may be born into a family of enlightened yogis. Such a birth is extremely difficult to obtain in this world.

6-43   *tatra tam buddhisamyogam*
                      labhate paurvadehikam
                      yatate ca tato bhuyah
                      samsidhau kurunandana

O Son of the Kurus (Arjuna), there he recovers the impressions of his former birth and with this he works hard for perfection.

The devotee that takes birth in the home of the pure and prosperous has to fulfill some harmless pleasures, before seriously continuing on his path to liberation. However, the one born in the yogi's family feels that he has already known the science of yoga. He is a born-yogi and this is a real rebirth.

6-44   *purvābhyāsena tenai 'va*
                      hriyate hy avaso 'pi sah
                      jijnāsur api yogasya
                      shabdabrahmā 'tivartate

By sheer force of habit, as it were, he is irresistibly attracted to yoga. Even the seeker of yoga transcends the Vedas.

The Vedas are guides for enjoyment in earth and heaven. They promote and prolong the cycle of death and rebirth. When the grace of God is received, intuitive or direct knowledge becomes the guiding force. Institutional guidance is no longer needed for perfection and liberation are in sight.

6-45   *prayatnād yatamānas tu*
                      yogi samsuddhakilbishah
                      anekajanmasamsiddhas
                      tato yāti parām gatim

The yogi, striving with perseverance, being free from any taint of sin through many cycles of birth, attains the highest goal at last.

The disciple has to struggle perhaps for many births before he reaches perfection. Constancy of the ideal in the midst of all situations reflect his true character. He has succumbed to the plan of God, namely, to redeem every soul through forgiveness, repentance or discipline of life. Even the ritualistic or most rebellious souls will have to succumb to this plan.

7-19
bahunām janmanām ante
jnānavān mām prapadyate
vāsudevah sarvam iti
sa mahātmā sudurlabhah

The wise devotee, at the end of many cycles of birth, finds refuge in Me, realizing the truth that Vasudeva is all. Rarest of all is such a noble soul.

Vasudeva here means the all-pervading consciousness. It is easy to say that God is everything. However, only a few, through experience have gained conviction of this. They are the true spiritual leaders of Society.

7-23
antavat tu phalam teshām
tad bhavaty alpamedhasām
devān devayajo yānti
madbhaktā yāni mām api

The fruits gained by these men of little understanding are temporary. Those who worship Indra and the other Gods reach them. But although the task is arduous those who strive for Me, be rest assured will taste of the eternal fruit of liberation.

In monastic Hinduism, one goes to the Lord and says "Let Thy Will be done", while in ritualistic Hinduism the disciple goes to the gods and goddesses and ask for specific worldly desires to be fulfilled. The difference is infinite bliss or temporary enjoyment.

8-5
antakāle ca mām eva
smaran muktvā kalevaram
yah prayāti sa madbhāvam
yati nā 'sty atra samshayah

And there is not the least doubt that whoever at the time of death, thinking of Me alone, giveth up this body and departeth, attaineth to My Being.

To be able to think of the Lord at the time of death requires a whole lifetime of preparation. Mukti, freedom from the compulsions of the cycle of birth and death is guaranteed if one thinks of the Lord at that moment.

8-6
yam yam vā 'pi smaran bhāvam
tyajaty ante kalevaram
tam tam evai 'ti Kaunteya
sadā tadbhāvabhāvitaḥ

O Son of Kunti (Arjuna), whatever state of being a man thinks of while leaving up his body, to that being does he attain, as he is always absorbed in that thought.

What we think we will become. Our past thoughts have determined our present birth and the present will determine our future.

8-7
tasmāt sarveshu kāleshu
mām anusmara yudhya ca
mayy arpitamanobuddhir
mām evai 'shyasy asamshayam

Hence thinkest always of Me and fight (do your duty). When thy mind and understanding are set on Me, unto Me alone shalt thou surely come.

The immediate duty of Arjuna was to fight. The fight is to maintain relation with his true divine-self. If he uses the excuse that he does not want to kill his kinsman, then it becomes an escapist attitude. Every duty secular or sacred must be surrendered to the Lord.

How the yogi relinquishes his body (8-10 to 8-13)(See color photo)

8-10
prayānakāle manasā 'calena
bhaktyā yukto yogabalena cai va
bhruvor madhye prānam āveshya samyak
sa tam param purusham upaiti divyam

He who does so, at the time of his departure, with a steady mind, devotion and strength of yoga setting firmly his life force in the centre of the eyebrows, attains to this Supreme Divine Person.

Yoga must be a life long practice for it to be practical at the time of death.

8-12   *sarvadvārāni samyamya*
              mano hrdi nirudhya ca
              murdhny ādhāyā 'tmanah prānam
              āsthito yogadhāranām

8-13   ***om ity ekāksharam Brahma***
              vyāharan mām anusmaran
              yah prayāti tyajan deham
              sa yāti paramām gatim

With all the gates of the body closed, the mind confined within the heart, his life-energy fixed in the head, engaged in firm yoga, uttering the monosyllable 'Om', Brahman, thinking of Me, he who departs, leaving the body, attains the Supreme Goal.(12 and 13)

The yogis' final exit from the body is like the river flowing into the vast ocean, his individual consciousness merging into the cosmic consciousness. First his body is made still, and then his senses are put to sleep. His mind then settles in his heart. The life force or prana (breathing) gets concentrated in the middle of the forehead, leaving the rest of the body cold. With the mind fully fixed on the absolute state of the Lord and the inaudible humming of the sound OM, the yogi finally exits as infinite bliss into the brilliance of the cosmic all pervading consciousness. (12 and 13)

State of no return (8-15 & 8-16)

8-15   ***mām upetya purnarjanma***
              duhkhālayam ashāshvatam
              nā 'pnuvanti mahātmānah
              samsiddhim paramām gatāh

These great souls, who have attained highest perfection, come to me, are no longer subject to rebirth, the ever-changing abode of sorrow.

Don't go to God for trivial things but instead seek to be an instrument in His hands, by surrendering to Him. He will then make you as Himself as He did with Sabari of the Ramayana and Praveer during the horse sacrifice in the Mahabharata.

8-16   *ābrahmabhuvanāllokāh*
                  punarāvartino 'rjuna
                  mām upetya tu kaunteya
                  punarjanma na vidyate

From the domain of Brahma down to this world all the seven worlds are
subject to cycles of birth, but, O Son of Kunti (Arjuna), having attained
Me, there is no rebirth.

*Including the abode of Brahma all planes of existence, or worlds are governed
by time, space and causation (creation). Brahma's abode is the last stage
before liberation. Here also the enjoyment seekers are reborn on earth but the
liberation seekers remain there until pralaya or the end of a day of Brahma
(incalculable years) and then they get liberated.*

8-18   *avyaktād vyaktayah sarvāh*
                  prabhavanty aharāgame
                  rātryāgame praliyante
                  tatrai 'vā 'vyaktasamjnake

At break of (Brahma's) day all embodied beings emerge from the
unmanifested. At (Brahma's) night fall, they merge into the same
unmanifested.

*The eternal cosmic play: creation, preservation and destruction of the universe are
all contained in the states of the mind of Brahma. Just as when one goes to sleep
all projections during wakeful state gets withdrawn. Likewise when Brahma (the
highest of individual souls) goes to sleep creation comes to an end.*

8-19   *bhutagrāmah sa evā 'yam*
                  bhutvā bhutvā praliyate
                  rātryāgame 'vashah pārtha
                  prabhavaty aharāgame

O Partha, this multitude of beings arising again and again fades away at
nightfall (of Brahma) and appears helplessly at daybreak (of Brahma).

*As man is a helpless creature of his own mind, because he cannot overcome
sleep, likewise he is, at the time of dissolution taken into the un-manifested
state. He may go through more than one of the days and nights of Brahma
before he gains liberation (or merges with the supreme self).*

8-21
avyakto 'kshara ity uktas
tam āhuh paramām gatim
yam prāpya na nivartante
tad dhāma paramam mama

That which is called the Unmanifested and Imperishable is the Supreme Goal. Having attained that from which there is no return (or rebirth). That is My Supreme Abode (highest state of Being).

When creation goes into the state of night it also becomes un-manifested but the beings return and continue from where they left off at the beginning of the next day. The beings that merge with the supreme God never return.

The path of light and darkness (8-23 to 8-26)

8-23
yatra kāle tv anāvrittim
āvrittim cai 'va yoginah
prayātā yānti tam kālam
vakshyāmi bharatarshabha

Now I shall tell thee, O Prince of the Bharata race, of the hour when yogins pass away not to return and of the time when they depart to return once more.

8-24
agnir jyotir ahah shuklah
shanmāsā uttarāyanam
tatra prayāta gacchanti
brahma brahmavido janāh

If men knowing Brahman depart during spells of the presiding Gods of fire, light, day, the bright half of the month or during the sun's northern course lasting six months, attain Brahman.

8-25
dhumo rātris tathā krishnah
shanmāsā dakshināyanam
tatra chāndramasam jyotir
yogi prāpya nivartate

The yogis who depart during spells of the presiding Gods of smoke, night, the dark half of the month or during the sun's southern course lasting for six months, attain the lustre of the moon and return (to this mortal world).

222
Eternal Answers

8-26

> *shuklakrishne gati hy ete*
> *jagatah shashvate mate*
> *ekayā yāty anāvrittim*
> *anyayā 'vartate punah*

Light and darkness are considered to be the eternal paths of the world. One leads to the ultimate goal of (man's) emancipation while the other causes his rebirth.

9-3

> *asraddadhānāh purushā*
> *dharmasyā 'sya paramtapa*
> *aprāpya mām nivartante*
> *mrityusamsāra-vartmani*

O Chastiser of Foes (Arjuna), men lacking in reverence for this faith do not attain to Me and wander about in the pathways of this mortal world.

Individuals who don't or who don't want to know this path of deliverance (moksha dharma) are destined to rebirth.

9-19

> *tapāmy aham aham varsham*
> *nigrihnāmy utsrijāmi ca*
> *amritam cai 'va mriytus ca*
> *sad asac cā 'ham arjuna*

O Arjuna, heat emanates from Me as I send down showers or withhold rain. I am both immortality and death. I am the cosmos revealed and unmanifested.

The Sun gives heat and the rays cause evaporation. Clouds are the source of rain. In like manner the Lord is the immortality of the Devas and death of the human beings. In the manifested He becomes the beings and in the unmanifested state He is the non-being or Consciousness.

9-20

> *traividyā mām somapāh putapāpā*
> *yajnair istvā svargatim prārthayante*
> *te punyam āsādya surendralokam*
> *ashnanti divyān divi devabhogān*

The adepts in the three Vedas who worship Me by performing sacrifices are cleansed of sin by drinking the soma juice. They pray to be received in heaven. They attain the holy domain of the king of heaven and savour of the pleasures of the Gods.

Study of the Vedas or drinkers of dew (soma) may obtain heaven but not liberation which is the goal of life.

The Vedas lead one to the path as described by this sloka and not union with the Cosmic Consciousness.

9-21   **te tam bhuktva svargalokam vishālam**
            kshine punye martyalokam vishanti
            evam trayidharmam anuprapannā
            gatāgatam kāmakāmā labhante

Having enjoyed the fruits of their desire in the spacious domain of heaven, they return to this world of mortals, when their store of merit is exhausted. Thus do the desire-ridden persons, following the rituals of the three Vedas, come and go.

It is said in the Vedas that seeking of fruits only, cause death and rebirth.

9-25   **yānti devavratā devān**
               pitrin yānti pitrivratā
               bhutāni yānti bhutejyā
               yānti madyājino 'pi mām

Worshippers of the Gods go to the Gods, ancestor-worshippers go to the manes, worshippers of the spirits go to the spirits and My worshippers come unto Me.

9-32   **mām hi pārtha vyapāsritya**
               ye 'pi syuh pāpayonayah
               striyo vaishyās 'tathā shudrās
               te 'pi yānti parām gatim

O Pārtha (Arjuna), women, Vaishyas, Sudras and the base-born are all sure to attain to the supreme goal, if only they take refuge in Me.

In ancient times, it was thought that the mind of man was more developed than women (except for a few). It was the same regarding Vaisyas (business class) and Sudras (working class). But the Lord refutes this by saying - all have the right for liberation. Untouchability, He dismisses totally. Take the case of Sri Rama using the services of Guha, a boatman from the so called low caste, to cross Him across the Ganges. Mother Sabari of the Ramayana the lowest of the low received liberation.

10-34

> *mrityuh sarvaharash cā 'ham*
> *udbhavas ca bhavishyatām*
> *kirtih shri vāk ca nārinām*
> *smritir medhā dhritih khsamā*

I am the all-devouring Death and am the source of future beings; among women, I am fame, prosperity, speech, memory, intelligence, firmness and forgiveness.

The supreme taking form as Brahma, Vishnu and Shiva, becomes the force of creation, sustenance and destruction (death). His grace goes to those who ardently seek it continuously. The qualities mentioned in this sloka are female qualities because of their grace and tenderness.

11-20

> *dyāvāprithivyor idam antaram hi*
> *vyāptam tvayai 'kena dishash ca sarvāh*
> *drishtvā 'dbhutam rupam ugram tave 'dam*
> *lokatrayam pravyathitam mahātman*

O Great Soul (Sri Krishna), the space between heaven and earth and all the quarters are filled by Thee alone. Seeing this wondrous, terrible form of Thine, the three worlds tremble in fear (just as I do).

12-7

> *teshāmaham samuddhartā*
> *mrityusamsārasāgarāt*
> *bhavāmi nacirāt pārtha*
> *mayyāveshitacetasām*

I rescue those who surrender all their actions to Me, meditate on Me, worship Me with single-hearted devotion and centre all their thoughts on Me, O Partha (Arjuna). I rescue these dedicated devotees before long from the ocean of mortal existence.

14-4   *sarvayonishu kaunteya*
murtayah sambhavanti yāh
tāsām brahma mahad yonir
aham bijapradah pitā

O Son of Kunti (Arjuna), whatever forms are born of wombs, great Prakriti is the womb and I am the father who plants the seed.

The gunas and death (14-15)

14-14   *yadā sattve pravriddhe tu*
pralayam yāti dehavrit
tado'ttamavidām lokān
amalān pratipadyate

When the embodied soul departs while sattva predominates, he attains to the bright regions of those who know the best.

The Sattvika person leaves the body in calmness and full consciousness.

14-15   *rajasi pralayam gatvā*
karmasangishu jāyate
tathā pralinas tamasi
mudhayonishu jāyate

He who dies while rajas predominate will be born among those attached to action and if he departs when tamas prevails will be born in the womb of stupid creatures.

The passionate (rajasika) person lives in excitement, sorrow and desires. When reborn he will be a person prone to excessive activity. The lazy (tamasika) man dies in unconsciousness state and takes rebirth as a subhuman.

14-18   *urdhvam gacchanti sattvasthā*
madhye tishthanti rājasāh
jaghanyagunavrittishthā
adho gacchanti tāmasāh

Those who abide in sattva go upwards (to higher realms), those who remain in rajas stay in the middle (this world), while the tamasic with their base traits (delusion etc.) sink downwards (to the underworld).

If the sattvika (happy) man is prone to pleasure, he will take rebirth as a celestial in the planes of little Gods. If he is bent towards knowledge, he will be reborn as a human. The passionate man remains a human of his current state while the dullards sink to lower world level.

14-20   ***gunān etān atitya trin***
                             dehi dehasamudbhavān
                             janma mrityu jarā duhkhair
                             vimukto 'mrtam asnute

The embodied one having crossed over these three gunas out of which the body is evolved, is freed from birth, death, decay and pain, and attains to immortality

Jivanmukta *– One who is free from body consciousness while dwelling in the body, has transcended the three gunas, the home of the Jivatman, the experiencer of birth, death and pain.*

15-8   ***shariram yad avāpnoti***
                             yac cā'py utkrāmati'shvarah
                             grihitvaitani samyāti
                             vāyur gandhāniva'shayāt

When the Lord of the body, that is, Jivātman, discards the body and enters into a different body, He takes these (the five senses and the mind) and moves on very much as the wind which carries off the particles of scents from their sources.

15-10   ***utkrāmantam sthitam vā 'pi***
                             bhunjānam va gunāvitam
                             vimudhā nā 'nupashyanti
                             pashyanti jnānacakshushah

Those who have lived a life enmeshed in materialism and have been ruled by the three tyrants - pleasure, pain and attachments, are the fools who fail to see Him when they leave this mortal coil at the time of death. But those who are turned inward see the Self with their wise eyes of knowledge.

The acquisition of intuitive faculty is the only means to know that God resides in one's body. Lack of it causes one to be controlled by external objects, the

mind and the intellect. This state, the individual can only experience only while travelling from body to body, birth after birth.

16-19
> **tān aham dvishatah krurān**
> **samsāreshu narādhamān**
> **kshipāmy ajarsram ashubhān**
> **āsurishv eva yonishu**

I mete out justice according to sin and merit. The sinful who are inimical to the seekers, cruel and unholy are the degraded ones whom I hurl back to the hell of this world.

Even God does not interfere with karma. "As you sow, so shall you reap".

16-20
> **āsurim yonimāpannā**
> **mudhā janmani janmani**
> **mām aprāpyai'va kaunteya**
> **tato yānty adhamām gatim**

Entering into demoniac wombs, the deluded ones, in birth after birth, without ever reaching Me, thus fall, O Kaunteya, into a condition still lower.

16-21
> **trividham narakasye'dam**
> **dvāram nāshanam ātmanah**
> **kāmah krodhas tathā lobhas**
> **tasmād etat trayam trajet**

Threefold is the gateway to this hell ending in damnation of soul - lust, greed and anger. Therefore, one should refrain from these.

Greed - *is to appropriate all objects of sense enjoyment exclusively to oneself. Anyone of these causes bondage let alone the three combined. These three are the originators of the demonical qualities.*

16-22
> **etair vimuktah kaunteya**
> **tamodvārais tribhir narah**
> **ācaraty ātmanah shreyas**
> **tato yāti parām gatim**

O Son of Kunti (Arjuna), once a man is set free from these, the three gates to darkness and practises what is good for his soul reaches the highest goal.

Ignorance is the root of all misery and the cause for hell on earth. One being under bondage of lust anger and greed is the lowest of a human being but when he breaks out of them his God ward progress is rapid.

16-23   ***yah shāstravidhim utsrijya***
                   vartate kāmakāratah
                   na sa siddhim avāpnoti
                   na sukham na parām gatim

He who casts aside the scriptural law and acts according to the promptings of his desire, does not attain either perfection or happiness or the supreme goal.

Following the scriptures one gains happiness and prepares himself for the supreme goal, liberation.

18-12   ***anistam istam misram ca***
                   trividham karmanah phalam
                   bhavaty atyāginām pretya
                   na tu samnyāsinām kvacit

The threefold fruit of action - evil, good and mixed - accrues after death to one who does not relinquish but there is none ever for the one who renounces.

The cycle of birth and death is a continuation based on the life one lives. Rebirth is dictated by and inherent in the type of characteristics of the previous lives. Beings of evil actions are first hurled into hell and then are reborn as beasts. Men of good actions enjoy heaven and then are reborn as heavenly bodies. While men of good and bad actions enjoy heaven and hell and are reborn in favourable environments. The noble ones that master the transmigration of birth and death (the perfect ones) exist as bodies but they are already established in the Self.

18-71   *shraddhāvān anasuyash ca*
                        shrinuyād api yo narah
                        so'pi muktah shubhāmllokān
                        prāpnuyāt punyakarmanām

If a man simply listens to this discourse with faith and without malice, he too, will be freed from his sins and repair to the heaven of the righteous.

Being an expert at academic explanation and not following it has no spiritual value. However, the person who listens to this discourse and follows even a little, will reap the appropriate fruit. The essence of religion lies in its practice and realization.

"Spirituality is not something to be gained by scriptural studies of hearsay. Mad indeed is the one who thinks of unravelling the mysteries of spiritual life with the help of a mind torn by passions, tyrannized by the senses and agonized by carnal hankerings" - Swami Pranavananda.

Foreign Associates

1. London Sevashram Sangha, 99-A, Devenport Rd. Shephred Bush, London W-12, 8 P.B., Ph. 0208-723-4257

2. Guyana Sevashram Sangha, Cove and John, East Coast Dem, Guyana, South America, Ph. 011-592-229-2721

3. Trinidad Sevashram Sangha 32 Nolan Street. Felicity, Chaguanas, Trinidad, (W.I.), Email: dibyanand@hotmail.com

4. Bharat Sevashram Sangha of NA (California) 2107, Albion Rd. R. R. 1, Rexale, Toronto M9W 5K7, Canada, Ph. (416) 798-0479, Fax: (416) 674-2734 Email: pushkarananda@yahoo.com

5. America Sevashram Sangha, Inc. 153-14, 90th Avenue, Jamaica Queens, New York -14432, Ph. 718-523-7515

6. Bharat Sevashram Sangha of NA 522 Garfield Ave Aurora ILL60506 Ph# 630-301-6039

7. Pranav Math :Bajiput, Madaripur, Khulna, Ashasuni, Naogaon, Dhaka, Bangladesh.

8. Fiji Sevashram Sangha GPO Box: 14064, Sauva, Fiji, Ph: (679) 330 2210 Email: fijisevashramsangha@rediffmail.com

9. Bharat Sevashram Sangha of North America, Inc (New Jersey) 3490 Route 27, Kendall Park, NJ 08824, Tel.#: 732-422-8880, Email: bssnanj@yahoo.com

10. Pranavananda Vidya Mandir, Kathmandu, Nepal

11. Bharat Sevashram Sangha of NA California 5600 Carbon Canyon Rd Brea CA 92823

OTHER ENGLISH PUBLICATIONS

The Prophet of The Age - By Swami Vedananda. Life & teachings of the great Acharya Srimat Swami Pranavanandaji, 230 pages.

Swami Pranavananda: The World-Teacher & Saint Saviour – By Dr. Prasanta Mukhapadhyay. The book presents a short but Penetrating review of the divine life of Swami Pranavanandaji Maharaj, the Architect and founder of Bharat Sevashram Sangha, 208 pages.

The Sangha Geeta - Divine Messages of the Great Acharya Srimat Swami Pranavanandaji Maharaj, founder of the Bharat Sevashram Sangha, 92 pages.

Ten Divine Messages of the Great Acharya Srimat Swami Pranavanandaji Maharaj – a philosophical study 92 pages.

Hindu Gods & Goddesses - Swami Nirmalananda. The book devotes to the general principles lying behind the concept of divine images and the general principles about the animals who carry the Gods. At the end of the book pictures of a number of images have been inserted to enhance the attraction of the book. Pages - 294.

Essence of Hinduism - by Dr. Durgadas Basu, in this book the author has adopted comparative method which characterizes his works on Law and Political Science. 133 pages.

Foundation of Religion - by a seeker, 138 pages.

The Divine Life-builder Swami Pranavananda - by Swami Vikashananda, 72 pages.

Reflections on Hinduism - by Yatiswaranada, 257 pages.

Re-organisation of India - by Swami Vedanandaji, 90 pages.

Illustrated Life – 'Pictorial' life sketch of Swami Pranavananda

The Making of An American Yogi – By Swami Parameshananda. The experiences over foreign monk with the activities of the Sangha and Swami Pranavanda.

Available From:
BHARAT SEVASHRAM SANGHA
211, Rash Behari Avenue
Kolkata – 700019 Ph. 2440-5178